HOW TO SCREW YOUR CUSTOMERS

Cover design by Green Talent Limited

Book design by Green Talent Limited

All rights reserved.

No part of this book may be reproduced in any form or by any electronic or mechanical means including information storage and retrieval systems, without permission in writing from the author. The only exception is by a reviewer, who may quote short excerpts in a review.

© Green Talent Ltd 2014

Visit our website at www.greentalent.co.uk

Printed in the United States of America

Copyright © 2014 Green Talent Ltd

All rights reserved.

ISBN-13: 978-1502357113

ISBN-10: 1502357119

DISCLAIMER

Although this is not a fiction book, and all stories and cases described have been experienced first hand by the author, due to possibly legal liabilities by companies who rather than learning may get upset, we must say that all characters, companies, etc. featured on this book are fictional, and any similarity with real companies or real people, is just by pure chance.

Logos and trademarks are used for reference only under the umbrella of fair use from the US trademark law and the Lanham Act, and are the sole property of the owners of the logos.

How to screw your Customers – Alfredo de la Casa

Contents

Introduction 8
Why me? Who am I? 10
The early years: Spain 12
Panrico 15
CCC 18
Gesco Informatica 20
MAPFRE 22
Banco Santander 24
Banco Santander, take 2 26
BBVA Bank 29
I had enough! I return to England 31
Job Centre 32
T- Mobile 34
Lloyds Tsb 36
Citibank 38
American Express 40
American Express 2 and Eclipse Computers .. 42
City Sprint Couriers 45
Easynet 47
Cable & Wireless 49
Orange 53
Three Mobile 57
Telefonica (Spain) 60

El Corte Ingles (Spain) 62
LG 63
Eroski Movil (Spain) 65
Hackney Council 67
Hackney Homes 69
British Telecom 71
British Gas 74
EDF 76
National Grid 77
Ryanair 78
Iberia 81
Iberia, part two 84
Thai Airways 87
Insure and Go 90
American Express Travel Insurance 92
Axa Insurance 94
HSBC Insurance 96
Rodizio Rico 98
Whetherspoons Birmingham Airport 100
Morrisons supermarkets 102
Santander 104
Santander, mortgages part 2 106
MBNA cards 108
1and1 110

5

Foreign and Commonwealth Office 112

Stanstead Express 114

London Buses 116

AOL (UK) 118

AOL part 2 120

Samsung 122

PC World 124

The Vietnam Times (but also suffering the wrong doing of Western companies) 126

Gaemmer Restaurant 127

Vietcombank 130

Techcombank 133

Sony 135

Amazon (UK) 137

Sony, part 2 139

Hai Long 5 Hotel (HCMC) 141

G2000 (Vietnam) 144

Coopmart (Vietnam) 146

X-O (Jarvis Investments) UK 148

Maximart (Vietnam) 150

Big C 152

Hoan My Hospital (Vietnam) 155

Vietnam Airlines 158

Vietnam Airlines Ground Services 161

Jet Star Pacific 163

Viet Jet Air..166

WHY NOT: how companies can do things better, much better, for their Customers, and indirectly for themselves…………………………………………………….. 172

Also from the Author……………………………….… 192

Introduction

I can not remember what was my first experience as a Customer, probably when I was born and I did not like coming out, feeling hungry, feeling cold, feeling so bad that I had to cry and scream.

Later on, and even now, I feel in a similar way due to the way which some companies and employees decide to treat me, the Customer, the person who brings them money and profit…I don't usually cry, but definitely I do scream!

The title plays with the double meaning of how to screw up your Customers, with many examples on how companies do this, but for each example I also offer an alternative way on how to screw the loyalty, and custom, of your Customers.

In this book I describe some real stories of what I have experienced, if not suffered, as a Customer, but this is not just about me complaining (I already did so to the companies, if not sued them), this book is about real examples of how not to treat Customers, and more important, I provide examples of how to deal in similar situations, pleasing the Customer without having to go bankrupt to do so, as usually, it is not that difficult, and it is easy to reach a win-win solution for both parties.

After many years lecturing on Customer Services, Business, and Business Communications, I am still astonished to see so many companies behaving badly.

In this book you will also find some examples, not so many unfortunately, of companies who do excel in treating Customers right, what they do to achieve this, and how do they deal with problems when they arise. It is a pity that so few companies decide to imitate them, as if they did, their profits would surely soar!

I want this book to be an easy to read, funny manual about Customer Services: for those who want to learn, what to do, what not to do, and how to deal with difficult situations, and more importantly, why to do so.

I hope you enjoy it, but if you don't, please email me (adelacasa@greentalent.co.uk) as I want to hear from you, and do something about it! An Amazon review is always welcome, even if bad, as it helps me to learn from my mistakes!

Alfredo de la Casa

Why me? Who am I?

I am a Customer for sure, so even though some companies don't believe it, I know better than anyone else what I want and how I want it!

From the Academic point of view, I have a degree in Business, Marketing and Economics, and I am a Chartered Management Accountant (CIMA) and a Certified Risk Practitioner.

I also have some other titles and diplomas, however you may be more convinced to keep reading, especially if apart from a funny read you are also looking to learn, if I tell you that I lecture in different International Universities: Marketing, Customer Services, Business Communications and more importantly, I deliver workshops and company training worldwide in these subjects.

I was born in London, England, but I have lived in different countries, giving me an excellent exposure to how companies do well, and how they don't, which is what I want to share with you, so let's begin!

Thanks to:

My wife, Thoa Kieu, who has suffered with me not only the wrong doing from many companies but also my bad tempered as a result.

To my many friends who have shared my frustrations, and have encouraged me to go ahead and fight, including:

Beatriz Gonzalez, Nitin Ravat, Paul Wallis, Saleh Ahmed, Ben Warner, Tanja Sturm, Myles Mcarthy, and many more.

And to all my Customers who have bought this and previous books, and who hopefully buy the next ones.

The early years: Spain

After being born, my parents moved to Spain, where they opened their business. Not an easy task, in the middle of a crisis in a country run by a dictator, but hard work, and knowing how to treat the Customers made them and their business very successful.

My dad did not go to university, or college, in fact he just went a few years to School. Being the eldest male in the family, his family could not afford to send him to school while his hands were needed to work the fields in a post war family who suffered hunger. However, like me, he spent his childhood in the family business, a bakery, where he learnt a lot until a fire burnt it up. The rest was self-taught.

I will not be making many book recommendations here, but even though it was published 30 years ago, I will always remember when I was gifted with a wonderful book: *In Search of Excellence, by Tom Peters and Robert Waterman.*

I was just a child and as usual, I went with my dad to the bank, where the Bank Director gave him a copy of the book; my dad was very busy running his business, and as he did not have time to read and I loved reading, he gave it to me.

I was around 13 then and a very avid reader, so I was happy and I went through the book in a weekend. However I was rather disappointed with it: the book described how the authors visited the most successful companies in America to know what made them successful, and one of the key things was treating Customers right… so obvious, everybody knows, so why write (and buy) a book about it, I wondered. Then I put the book in my library, that I would then read again a few years later and be fascinated by it.

And my childish mind was right: **isn't it obvious that if you want to make business you should treat your Customers well?** I think it is, plain common sense, however why does it happen so little?

I wonder the answer is a combination of lack of professional training in Customer Services/Business and the "mind obstruction" of seeing the tactical "money now" rather than the strategic "Customers for life"

Customers buy our products and services, give us profit, they recommend our products, keep buying our products,… in other words they pay our salaries and make companies and shareholders rich. So, shouldn't we try to treat them as well as we can, and be thanked for their business?

Ok, may be not all the Customers are great, some of them can be a pain (surely many companies have me in such category), but aren't the majority just nice people, helping us to succeed? How many out of how many try to cheat us? In reality hardly any. How many have unreasonable requests? Very few, and more important, those with what appear as having unreasonable requests… do they have a valid reason to feel that way?

From Restaurants to hotels, banks, insurance companies, Government departments, airlines, transport companies,… the list is endless, why screw your Customers rather than nurture them?

Panrico

Panrico has been a bakery leader in Spain for many years. In the 70s and 80s, Panrico and its competitors worked hard to promote, especially via television advertising, small cakes aimed to school children.

One of these promotions matched some of the, at the time current cartoons: if you bought so many cakes and sent the coupons to Panrico, you would receive a toy.

Although I remember the cakes being delicious, we children were motivated by obtaining the little toy, so when I finally reached the amount of coupons needed I was very excited to get the toy.

My mum mailed the coupons and the form, and we waited and waited, but nothing ever arrived. I clearly remember waiting for the postman every day, and the enthusiasm soon resulted in disappointment.

I asked my mum never to buy those cakes for me again, and she offered to write a letter to Panrico.

Surprisingly, they replied to the letter, answering that as they never received the coupons I could not have the toy. To which my mum wrote again informing Panrico that if we did not receive our toy by the end of the month, she would write to the newspapers and radio stations informing how Panrico was cheating Customers. In less than a week the toy with an apology letter arrived.

I accept that my letter may have gone astray in the mail, however I was not the only child in my school under that situation, so unlikely.

Nevertheless, how many Customers are likely to cheat and demand they have sent something when they haven't? In my experience, very few do so. So is it really the best option to refuse the prize, risking losing real Customers and bad publicity, especially if the cost of the prize is insignificant? The answer is a rotund NO.

It is a shame that the only way we could get what we wanted is via threats. By then companies have usually lost the Customer.

WHAT IF: what if, Panrico on receipt of my mum's first letter had answered on the lines of "Sorry to have kept you waiting for your toy, but we did not receive your coupons. Nevertheless as we value you as a Customer, here is your toy!

By doing this, they would have reinforced so much my, and my mum's loyalty to Panrico. Instead we got angry, stop buying their products, and shared our

"experience" with other mums and school children… try to measure the effect.

CCC

CCC was one the most famous distance learning course providers in Spain, who was heavily advertising in both TV and printed media.

As a teenager I was curious about what profession to choose for my future career, so I filled an information request and sent it to receive information about several courses which at the time did sound interesting.

I received the information via mail catalogue, studied it and put it apart to read again when the time to choose my career arrived.

A few weeks later a representative of CCC rang to my parents asking to speak to me regarding the courses. When my mum told him that I was very young and that I would not be buying any course, he bursted and shouted to my mum that she should educate me better and stop wasting his time and money ordering information about products I would not buy.

This was unpleasant and when I arrived home I was told off by my mum, and instructed never to request information from them (or others) again.

So this company encourages and encourages people to request information, which is what I did, and then because I am too young to buy… complain and shout to my mother… what the hell! What message are they giving? Terrible! I can not imagine anyone knowing trusting such a company with their education.

WHY NOT: once they rang and found out that I was too young, why not give their personal details and encourage my mum to contact them once I was old enough to do these courses.

They would have created a good image, rather than a terrible one, plus I would have had a good memory of this company, and something to look forward, rather than put them in my "black list", and over 30 years after, I have not forgotten!

Gesco Informatica

Once in University, one of my dreams came true, and I managed to save enough money to buy my first Macintosh computer and printer.

I was very proud and bought one of the latest models from Gesco Informatica, one of the authorised Apple dealers in my city, who offered free installation service.

They came to my home, installed the Mac, the printer and left.

This was my second computer, but my first printer and I was excited, so I just wrote something for the sake of printing but the printer did not print.

Quite disappointed I rang Gesco Informatica, who refused to send the technician because they thought it was my fault and that I was doing something wrong, so I had to get the printer and carry if with me to the shop, and printers were heavy then!

Once in the shop they checked the "brand new printer" and it did not print. I asked for a new one, but they refused to give me one, and asked me to wait for the faulty one to get repaired.

Give or take, I had to wait over a month to get my "new" printer repaired: unacceptable.

WHY NOT: test the printer and everything and make sure all works before leaving.

Why not send the technician to the Customer's home, rather than annoy the Customer with bringing the product to the company? I know is easier and cheaper for the company, however who is serving who?

Why not replace the printer immediately, the Customer paid for a working one! So rather than transfer the problem to the Customer, accept it, and make him happy, that is the quality he (I) paid for!

MAPFRE

Unfortunately my mac did not last long. Not a problem with the computer, but on a stormy night, a lighting came through the phone lines, blow the modem and the Mac's motherboard... I was devastated!

Fortunately, my dad had a very comprehensive home insurance that covered all home appliances if damaged by lightning, among other things.

However when my dad rang his insurance agent, with who he had a long business relationship and many insurance policies, he just sent an "expert" to our home, who after carefully inspection, confirmed the lighting and its effects in my Mac and modem.

However before they agreed to replace it, they insisted that I got several quotes from experts for both computer and modem, stating the price of repair, nature of repair and how much would be a new one.

Once more the company, who is the one who has the problem, decides to pass it to the poor Customer, in this case me: so I had to get all devices, go to different shops, explain the situation to them, ask for an inspection and then a formal report for the insurance company.

Some of the shops/technicians were nice enough to do it. However when I provided the written quotes to the insurance company, they insisted that I asked the technicians for a copy of their professional certificates confirming that they were qualified to do their job…I had had enough!

So, as the claims expert was the most inflexible person on earth, or close to, I told my dad about the issue, and how embarrassed I was to go and ask the technicians for that. He found an easy solution: he called the insurance agent and requested to cancel every single insurance policy he had with them.

The agent, obviously earning good commission through the many policies my dad had for his different businesses and properties, was shocked and asked my dad to wait 24 hours.

After this, he convinced the claims expert to accept my claim and get the devices repaired.

WHY NOT: deal with the repairs yourself? If you don't trust the Customer, why don't use your own approved technicians rather than pass the ball to the Customer and ask to do work for you for free?

Banco Santander

I started being a Customer of Santander at early age, and I had so many bad experiences with them that made cancel my accounts.

Due to a twist of destiny, Santander buying my beloved Abbey National, I am still a Santander Customer, and as we speak, I am waiting for their Complaints Department to answer to me, 10 days so far, but more about this later in the book, as Santander is probably one of the worst Customer Service Offenders I have come across.

Back to Spain, I had two issues with them. As a university student they were offering a very tempting interest rate to students if they opened a student account, so I decided to open one and moved my little savings to the red giant.

Having the interest paid monthly, I was waiting to see if they would really pay what they promised, and obviously they did not.

So after carefully checking my calculations several times, I went to the branch and I was ready to complain. The branch manager was looking at me rather ironically, and told me several times that the interest was calculated automatically by the computer and that therefore it was right and I was wrong.

It was a very small amount, but for me it was a matter of principles, and I did not like being embarrassed in front of the bank staff, so I insisted, and finally the bank manager asked someone to prove me on paper that I was wrong.

So after a while and many consultations, I was told that they would need to speak to the head office and come back to me with an answer.

A few weeks later I received a letter saying that due to some internal error my interest had been wrongly calculated, and would soon be credited in my account.

WHY NOT apologise? Why not listen to the Customer and start from the base that the Customer is (always) right?

Just because I was young it does not mean that they know better than me, but even if they did, they should still respect me as a Customer.

Banco Santander, take 2

A couple of years later, my "friends" from Santander would be themselves again, and make withdraw all my money.

One day I went to use my debit card and withdraw some money, when I discovered that I had no money, and in fact the statement was even showing a negative statement.

There was no internet banking or internet fraud those days, so I had no idea what the issue was, so armed with the mandatory photo id I went to the bank to investigate.

The bank teller, in a rather dry manner told me that the issue was obvious: I should not spend more money than I had, and as I had spent more I was "in the red", so why was I wasting their time.

Still young and inexperienced, I did not give him the slap that he deserved, so I asked him to explain to me how that had happened as I was sure I had not overspend.

He was rather reluctant to show me and asked me to wait for the arrival of my monthly statement by mail, where everything would be detailed. I told him that doing so was not good enough, and that I needed to access my money, to which he replied I had no money.

As a result my voice started to raise to the point that all Customers around clearly heard me when I shouted that Santander was nothing but a bunch of criminals and that I would not leave until I got my money or an explanation, and that he was welcomed to call the police. Moment in which, the branch director called me in his office, not really to solve the problem but to stop me to upset the other Customers.

It took him under 10 seconds to bring my records on screen, and see the issue: I did not have enough money because I had been paying for goods via 5 cheques for a higher value than I had in the account.

When I told him that there must had been an error because that was not possible, he replied that computers make no mistakes, and that everything was correct.

Although I appreciate that computers don't usually make mistakes, or hardly ever do, people using them do, and as I told him, may be I was too stupid, but how come I could have paid something by cheque, using a student account that did not issue cheque books, and when they have never issued me a cheque book. He went back to the computer, and went pale when he realised I had a student account.

I was sent home, and asked to wait for the result of the investigation, which took two more weeks. Apparently "someone" had made a mistake, and charged some cheques from my cousin to my account, and they assured me that the money would be refunded.

Although the money was refunded I had since received several charges for unauthorised overdraft, so I had to go again to the bank, have another verbal fight, in order to get those charges refunded, as the reason for the overdraft usage was Santander charging me for cheques from someone else.

Once I had all my money back I decided to go once again and cancel my account; I was not even asked why.

WHY NOT treat Customers with respect to start with, and take the few seconds that it takes to check the statement in the computer and give an explanation.

Someone, not the Customer, made a big mistake, there was no apology, and no compensation or goodwill gesture for the time or stress caused.

BBVA Bank

Having left Santander Bank, I still had banking needs, so I opened a current account with BBVA bank, where I was assured that I did not have to pay any banking charges as long as I kept a minimum balance; it sounded logic and good.

However within the first month I had to visit the bank twice, and not in a good mood!

My first visit was when I received my first statement and some admin fee was charged to my account, I enquired as I had been told I had no banking charges to be told that it was not a banking charge but an "admin" charge to cover the cost of sending me the statement every two weeks by mail.

As I did not need one, I requested the statements to be cancelled, but that was not possible.

The second visit was after I received another statement this time with a rather hefty charge. I was told that the reason was that they were issuing me with a bank card, which I had not requested, and when I asked for it to be cancelled I was told it was not possible.

WHY NOT: explain clearly any charges to Customers, rather than bleeding them in as many ways as possible?

With such short term view, it is not abnormal that so many people change banks!

I had enough! I return to England

By then I was in my mid twenties and I had had enough of being treated like rubbish by companies, so I decided to follow one of my dreams and go to live where I was born: England.

I had visited England before as a teenager and I was fascinated, so with the huge criticism of friends and family for leaving a job as Purchasing Director to go to England with nothing, I decided to make a move.

I left my job, and I was ready to move to a country where Customer was King, or so I thought…

Job Centre

As I had been working in Spain for a while and making big money, I was entitled to some generous benefits from the Spanish Government, so I did all paperwork, and once in London I took it to the Job Centre, where I had to fill even more forms, for them to claim directly from the Spanish Government. I was asked to return in two weeks, and so did I.

After two weeks I was asked to return after another two weeks, but I was growing impatient because I had a time frame by when I had to claim my money in order not to lose it, and I told so to the Job Centre employee.

Two weeks later, there I was again, and guess what, I was asked to return in two weeks time, but this time I requested to speak to a manager, who explained to me what the problem was: because they were not clear about the exact address that was in the stamp of my Spanish documentation, they were holding it… that was the fuel that made me exploit and with a heavy punch to the desk, in the very traditional way of dealing with civil servants, I shouted "You moron! Don't you realise that there is no address on the stamp, as the address is on the heading, and if you don't process the papers I will lose my money. Which can of idiot are you who waits four weeks to find out the non-existent address on a stamp"

They were not expecting such reaction, so a higher level manager came to "deal" with me. She listened to me, apologised for the misunderstanding, and guaranteed that the form would be processed within 48 hours.

This was my first and last interaction with the Job Centre. But with such bunch providing such unprofessional service, cant hey really help anyone to get a job? I doubt it very much.

WHY NOT acknowledge the importance of timed documents. If they did not know what the address was, why not ask for help from the Customer rather than ask the Customer to return after two weeks and do nothing about it during such time, why not deal with the issue.

What would have happened if I had lost my money due to their incompetence?

T·· ·Mobile·

T- Mobile

I bought my first mobile and contract in England from T-Mobile, to who I paid a monthly fee that gave me some "free" minutes; I signed a direct debit form that guaranteed that every month the phone company would get the money from my bank directly, so I had nothing to worry about.

Ten months down the line, I tried to make a call but the phone was not working, so I phoned the help service who transferred me to the Accounts department where I was told that I could not make calls because I had not paid my last bill, and therefore, and without prior warning they had disconnected me.

My reply was clear: I was paying by direct debit, I had money in my bank account, how come the last bill could be unpaid, and why they had disconnected me without even calling me?

The person told me that they did not have any direct debit in my account and that I was wrong. So I asked him to check how the prior 10 months payments had been taken. After a few minutes he said…hmmm yes you paid by direct debit.

As I told him, I could not delete the direct debit from their systems, so why was I being punished? I was then told that they had had a new system installed and may be that was the reason. By then I had been over 40 minutes on the phone, paying for a call, so I asked for a solution, and I was told to be paid by credit card plus a £2 premium.

Why should I pay a premium for something I was not responsible for? He told me to contact Customer Services, which I did, which resulted in me wasting more time and money. The following day I changed to another phone company.

WHY NOT: even if a Customer does not pay the last bill, why not ring him, at least to warn him/her are discontinuing the service?

Why punish a Customer, for something he is not at all responsible for.

Lloyds TSB

One of the problems when you move to a new country is that you don't have any credit history, so simple things like opening a bank account can be a real nightmare.

When I relocated to the UK, I brought with me two official letters of recommendation, in English, from my two Spanish Banks. However it proved to be a nightmare when I tried to open a bank account to put my cash in.

The worst offender was Lloyds TSB. When I tried to open the account I was told that to do so I would need to pay £200 to check my credit with the Spanish banks.

Even though I told them that I just wanted to put cash in and not to borrow, they did not care, and when I showed them the letters of recommendation from my banks and asked why I need to pay when they already had the information from my banks, I was told that they did not trust me and they needed to check by themselves, and charge me for the service. I was speechless!

WHY NOT trust a Customer, I was not asking for credit, or even a credit card, I was just asking for a basic account to put my money, in fact a rather large amount of money. Why not trust the officially signed and stamped Bank letters?

Years later the same bank would approach me on a regular basis offering bank accounts, credit cards, loans, mortgages, everything... but I did not forget how I was treated by them, and I will never will!

Citibank

I was convinced by Citibank Spain to take one of the cards, and when I moved to England I took it with me.

As I was having problems to open a bank account and build my credit history in England, I could not get a local credit card, so as Citibank was present in England I approached them for help.

The UK branch told me that as I was a Customer of the Spanish branch I should deal with them. When I called the Spanish branch and asked them to transfer my card to the UK, they refused, because although they were an international bank, they were separate companies and I should understand, well I did not1

WHY NOT help your Customer? The UK branch could easily access my banking records in Spain for building my credit scoring or ask the Spanish branch for my credit scoring... it was easier to do nothing and not Care for the Customer.

Soon after I cancelled my card, and I have not done any business with Citibank since.

American Express

Although not a frequent user at the time, I subscribed to an American Express green card once I was living in Spain.

Several times I hesitated whether it was worth paying a rather high fee for a credit card, which was not accepted in many places, especially considering that I already had many other cards which were not only widely accepted but free.

The answer came when I moved to London. After having been terribly disappointed with the "treat" from Citibank, I decided to burn my last chance and try the same with American Express, honestly I was not expecting much, I was not expecting anything at all.

So I rang their helpline in England, and after having given my card details and pass security, the first question from the phone operator really surprised me: "Sir, it appears in our records that you got your card in Spain, but you are calling in England, would you like me to transfer the call to someone who can serve you in Spanish?" Wow! They still do not know what I want and they are already trying to make my life easier.

After talking to them about my issue in England, they told me that unfortunately they could not transfer my card to England, however as they had my Customer details from Spain, they could issue me with a new English card, and it was up to me whether I decided to keep or cancel the Spanish one.

Oh my god, I was astonish to finally come across to someone who really understood what Customer Service is about, and what running a business is about.

My positive experience would not finish there, when I asked how long to receive my new card I was told that they could mail it and would be with me within two to three days, or alternatively I could pass by their offices in central London that day after 3pm…which I did, and my new card was there waiting for me.

If meeting Customers' expectations is great, exceeding them is definitely the way to Customer loyalty and succeed in business.

This would not be my only positive experience from American Express, and the fact is that 18 years after, I am still a loyal Customer.

American Express 2 and Eclipse Computers

Several months after my arrival, it was time to buy a new computer, and the new colourful i-mac was released at the time, so after doing some price comparison I decided to buy my new imac from Eclipse Computers who would deliver in two days and who gave a lot of guarantees including one year full home repair guarantee.

I had to wait a bit longer to receive it because the delivery company, Citysprint, gave terrible service (see next chapter for further details).

So after collecting the computer I installed it in my room, to discover that the modem was not working. I tried everything, all sort of tests, but there was no way to connect to the internet.

So I called the company who put me through the technical helpdesk and made me run twice every single test I have already run and which I had already told them that I had already run.

So once they finally were convinced that the computer had a problem, they ask me to return it to their premises, however I told them that their terms stated, and in fact was a selling point for me, that they offered a full year on site technical support and repair, and that therefore I wanted them to send me a technician.

Their reply was that the earliest they could send me a technician was 7 weeks from them, and therefore it may be better if I contracted and pay for a courier service to deliver the computer to them and that I was also liable to pay for re-delivery to my address.

Needless to say that I was fuming, I felt cheated, and after talking to several employees I got exactly the same response. Frustrating!

I was lucky to have paid the computer with my American Express card, so I decided to give them and call and see if they could help, and they did.

They listened to my problem, and then American Express impressed me again when the Customer Service representative told me not to worry, that at the same time as we were speaking he was crediting my account with the amount I paid, and that from that time the problem was no longer mine but theirs. He kindly asked me to send him an email confirming our conversation, and that he would be in touch with an update. What else could I ask for?

The following day I received a call from American Express asking me to pack the computer and get it ready to be delivered to an address they gave me, and to tell him which day and time would be convenient for a courier to pick it up.

He also told me that after speaking to the company they offered to send another computer, but that I could also choose for a full refund, which I did. Everything went smoothly and I bought my next imac from a local retailer.

WHY NOT honour what you say and offer "real" on site service. Who would be willing to wait seven weeks, or even seven days to have a computer repaired?

Why pass the responsibility and even costs to the Customer when he is not responsible for anything apart from giving his money and business to a rogue trader? Eclipse computers ended up losing an order, losing a Customer, paying for couriers, and probably blacklisted by American Express.

On the other hand American Express reinforced the satisfaction of a Customer by once more exceeding his expectations, a Customer who has been recommending Amex ever since.

City Sprint Couriers

Next day delivery service is expensive, and when people decide to pay for it, especially when other cheaper options are available, is because they urgently need or want the delivery.

When I bought my imac I was anxious to have it, and I even took one day off work to wait at home and receive it. I dint!

After waiting all day home, waiting for the delivery, I decided to ring at 5pm to the courier and enquiry about my packet. I was surprised to hear that "according to their records" they had attempted delivery twice but there was no one home…what the F@@$?

It made no difference when I told them politely that I had been home all day and no one has attempted delivery or when I accused them of being useless liars. They told me I had two options, to wait for the next day and be home, which I couldn't do, or go to their depot and pick it up.

They could not care less, even when I pointed to them that I did not have a car and that their depot was just 2 km away, they did not care, great!

So I decided to walk there and to my surprise I was told on arrival that I could not pick it up without having a delivery card.

Had the person on the phone mentioned delivery card, or anything, obviously not. So another door was closed on my way to get my imac, however I was resilient and after explaining my issue once more I told them that they had three options:

1.- To give me my packet.

2.- Call the police.

3.- Expect me to sleep there.

I got my packet, but they refused to call me a taxi, as it was not their job to do so…

Since then, every time I have ordered something online I have requested not to be delivered with this company.

WHY NOT deliver on time, which is why you get extra money.

Why lie to the Customer? Why create more problems for the Customer rather than solve them?

#easynet

Easynet

Easynet was one of the main internet providers in England once I was living there, so considering the various options available I decided to give them a try, it was not easy!

I contracted the services online, feeling a series of forms, entered my payment details, click, click, click and blank screen… not a good start for an internet company.

So unsure of whether I had or not contracted the service I decided to wait a couple of hours, after which, as I had received no confirmation email, and after having failed to get Customer support on the phone I decided to go again through the registering process. This time all went well.

My surprise would arrive at the end of the month once I was charged twice for the service. When I enquired they told me that I have contracted two of the same service.

I explained to them what happened on the day of registration, which they did not care about. They also did not "understand" that no-one would ever contract the same service twice for the same address under the same phone line, as it is obvious that no one can use or need the same internet service twice at the same time… they did not care, so I paid the first month twice and cancel the service.

WHY NOT ensure the registration system works, and if problems arise, when they don't?, listen to the Customer and use the logic to assess whether the claim is or is not reasonable.

They had 2 months of my custom, and never again more, plus zero recommendations to friends, but the opposite.

Why so often do companies employ people with zero Customer Service skills and below zero communication skills in roles with direct contact with Customers? I wonder…

NTL

At some point I decided to move flats and get closer to my job at the time, so after renting a new place with no phone or internet connection I decided to employ the services of the cable company NTL (Cable and Wireless), who at that time was advertising as having the fastest internet service, and best Customer service of the country.

So after booking the service and agreeing the date, an engineer came and put a box and a connection in the room. I was so happy with the service that I started recommending it.

A few months later, both the phone and internet would stop working with no warning, and after spending a fortune on my mobile phone to call Customer Services (as the landline was not working), I managed to get all sort of excuses of why the service did not work.

After talking to several people, for what it ended up in an hour longer conversation, it was agreed that 3 days later in the morning an engineer would come to repair the problem.

Three days felt like and awful long time to wait, but it was the best I could manage to arrange after tough negotiation. I had to take time off work to be at home, and on the key day

How to screw your Customers – Alfredo de la Casa

I waited patiently from 8 am, waiting and waiting for the repair man to come and save my life.

Having been given the slot from 8 am to 2pm (is really six hours the best schedule management these companies can achieve, or is it that they simply don't care and they just look after themselves?), I waited and waited and at 2pm, having been stood up I rang Customer Services to complain, and to unfortunately find out that the engineer was very busy and therefore had to cancel my appointment.

What the f...? Why, assuming that it was true, they had not called me in advance? Their reply was that they did not know, and I was offered an alternative date same time two days later.

Same story repeated itself, however this time I called at 1.45 to be told that the engineer was already in my road and it would take him 10 minutes to reach me.

An obvious lie, and as I told the operator, how can someone who is already on my road, a road barely 500 metres long, needs 10 minutes, especially considering that I had free parking by my door.

You may have guessed that the 10 minutes turned into almost three hours, but at the end someone arrived and solved the problem, or so we thought.

Happy having back internet and phone I tried to catch up with work, to be interrupted by several calls in a foreign language, many of them in the early hours of the day.

At some point I got a call from someone threatening me to go to the police because I had stolen his number…

So I made a new call to NTL who confirmed that the engineer may have made a mistake, and that as a result they needed to disconnect my line, and arrange a new visit, three days later of yet another engineer. I was speechless.

You would have expected that after such cock up, a company would have given priority to the fault and send someone immediately, but nope, and in fact they stood me up again, making me waste another day of work.

I filed a formal complaint with the company, in fact I filed many, to after a month be called by one of the directors' secretary and offer me £10 compensation.

I felt outraged! I asked her about how would she feel if someone stole 6 working days from her and was offered just £10 compensation, to be told by her that it did not matter because that was the maximum I would get.

After suggesting her where she could stick her generous offer, I cancelled my contract with NTL, I contacted BT and file a legal case against NTL, which I won.

WHY NOT: why not inform the Customer of any changes in any agreement, it has been a long time since doctors can give 15 minute slots to patients, so why Customers are forced to take days off work, not being able to leave their houses, simply because these rogue

companies decide to take the easy way, not to mention when there is no wrong doing from the Customers.

Why lie to Customers and treat them as if they were stupid? And if things go pear shape, why not compensate Customers fairly for the damage done.

Had I been offered £150-200 I would have been satisfied, but £10? What an insult! At the end the company ended paying me a couple of thousands, not to mention their legal costs.

Orange

After having been several years having Orange as my mobile phone provider, and happy with them, one day I was surprised to arrive home and find two packets from Orange containing each, a new phone with a new number.

I rang their Customer service department, and after waiting for a while and having described the situation to three employees, I was finally transferred to someone who did show interest to solve the problem; he took notes and told me that he would investigate and ring me in the next 2 to 3 days.

As no one ever rang me back, and being a bit tired of seeing the packages every day, I rang Orange again. I had to tell the story several times again, but this time I was told that as the 7 day grace period had passed, I could no longer return the phones, and I had to pay the subscription for the two phones for the following two years.

It did not matter how many times I told this person that I had nor ordered nor signed for any subscription, he kept telling me that I should have thought it twice before ordering two expensive phones, and that now I had no other option than to pay the monthly subscription. I was shocked.

I decided to go to an Orange shop and try my luck face to face. So after locating the nearest store and asking for the manager, who was quite understanding, she told me she could not take the phones as I had not bought them from her shop, however she called and put me through someone in Customer Services.

After having told the story once more, I was told that I could return the phones, and then I was told that the courier company would contact me for a convenient time for pick up, problem solved or so I thought!

I was also passed to the finance department who told me that as they had no formal notification of me cancelling the two lines (which I had not ordered!) I would be billed £90 plus the cost of my current line, so they suggested that I cancelled my direct debit, and that I should pay my normal bill until the issue was solved, it made sense, and so I did.

When the courier company rang they insisted to pick up the packets from 9 to 5, and refused to pick it up from my office address, such flexibility! So I told them that I would not take a day off work just to suit them, and I was told that it was my problem.

At that point I had the feeling that this would not have a happy ending, so I decided to check with my lawyer, who confirmed that under the Sale of Goods Act, and considering that there was no wrongdoing from my part, I actually had nothing to do but to inform the company of the problem, which I already had done, and they were responsible to arrange a convenient time (for me) to have the phones picked up.

I rang Orange, emailed them and faxed, several times, but no response. Until one day that I try to make a call with my mobile, and I could not.

So I rang Orange to see what the problem was, to be told that my line had been suspended because I had no paid the outstanding bills.

Needless to say that I explained the situation to the person, and to her manager, but they told me that it was my problem and not theirs, that I would not recover my line until I paid the full bill (I had already pay for my line, but not for the other two), and if my story was right I could later claim the money back…

I did a little research, chose a new mobile provider and moved on.

Monthly bills from Orange kept arriving, and at some point they were paired with threats of legal action against me. So after filling several complaints in writing, to which I never received a reply, I decided to take Orange to court.

I won the case, compensation and an apology, while Orange lost a Customer and money.

WHY NOT: try to solve the problems of a loyal Customer, listen to him, and try to do what is right.

Why not try to investigate and see whose fault is it, and in any case try to solve the situation and care about the Customers, who are actually paying the salaries of the employees?

By the way, it was never clarified who had ordered the phones, as Orange was unable to provide any proof of me or anyone else having even placed an order...

Three Mobile

With no many options available, and considering that I had already been really disappointed by two major mobile carriers, I decided to move with Three Mobile, a new one in the market, with who I partnered for a few years.

Unfortunately things could not last long, and even though I had even opened a second contract, this time for a usb modem with internet line, I had to cancel and sue them.

When it was time to renew my year contract, I was called by a Three mobile representative who offered me a new phone, plus 12 months of unlimited internet if I renewed for 18 months. It was such a fantastic offer that I took it.

I soon received my new phone, with reliable internet access, however when my first bill arrived I was charged by internet usage.

How to screw your Customers – Alfredo de la Casa

I called Customer Services, who told me that they did not see any free internet service in my account, and asked me to pay the bill and leave it with them, and they would ring me back within 24 hours.

You guessed it! No one ever rang again, so I had to go through a new Three Mobile agent, who, this time could see that I had 12 months free internet in my account but who told me that because I had used the internet too much I had to pay.

What? I told him that I had unlimited internet, so how come I had to pay, especially considering that I just used the phone to access my email? His answer really blew my mind: their unlimited internet package had a limit of 50 MB per month.

I entered an endless discussion with him and his manager about the meaning in English of the word "unlimited", but I lost the battle, as according to them, something which was unlimited could still be limited in number…

Several similar conversations followed, and many times I threated them verbally and in writing with stop paying the bills, but they did not care, so I stop paying my bill. Three days later, while I was overseas, both my line and my modem service, even though I had continue to pay for the latter, stopped working.

Several expensive international calls lead me to discover that although I had paid every bill for several years on time, the moment my account had an unpaid bill for three or more days, all the services were cancelled.

I was fuming, and on my return to England the conversations and emails continued, but I was ignored, Three Mobile continued to bill me on a monthly basis for services that they were not allowing me to use, while ignoring my complaints.

Another legal battle, this time via Ombudsman which resulted in an agreement of contract termination.

WHY NOT: deliver what you promise to the Customers, or stop over selling services, or actually cheating, people are not stupid!

Why not return calls when you promise to do so, why ignore emails and faxes.

And more important, in a market with many providers, if you stop a service, especially a service which costs you nothing, as a result of the Customer withholding payments because he is being ignored, do you think that anyone would pay, when they can simply go to another supplier?

I moved to Vodafone, with who many years after I keep a contract with, without a single problem!

Telefonica (Spain)

As I was flying to Spain on a regular basis, and visiting friends and family, I decided to get a Spanish mobile, and I chose the national carrier, as it had a good reputation.

I bought the phone, a LG (see later), on the most reputable retailer, El Corte Ingles (see later).

Happy with my new phone, with a pay as you go contract, I was shocked when a couple of months later I returned to Spain and I could nor make nor receive calls.

I called their offices who told me that as I had not used the phone for a month they had cancelled my number, and actually given it to another person.

I was fuming that no one has told me in advance about such restriction, and as my phone was locked on that network, I bought a new sim card, but I was totally unhappy, not to mention that by cancelling my line they also took away all my money, which I suspected was not very legal.

WHY NOT: If there is a restriction in a contract, why not inform the Customer in advance, and let him decide whether to accept it or not. Business will go only so far if Customers feel being cheated.

El Corte Ingles (Spain)

This Spanish retailer has always been associated with good quality products and great service, hence people like me decide to pay more at their outlets, as in theory, the Customer Services experience is better.

After having bought a phone two months before and bought a new sim card, I spent part of my 5 day break trying to make a call to discover that the phone was broken.

So I took it back to the store where I bought it to be told that as I had bought it more than one month ago, they could do nothing, even though it was under guarantee, and that I had to take it to the manufacturer myself, and that I would be given no replacement.

WHY NOT: take responsibility for the products you sell. Customers can deal directly with the manufacturers, but so can you, and at the end of the day you are making the profit, remember Customers can also take their business somewhere else, and we do!

LG

I took the two month old (used for five days) phone to the manufacturer, LG, who refused to replace it, and who asked me to wait two to three weeks to repair.

They did not care that I was going to be in the country just for a few days, they refused to lend me a phone, give me a new one, let me take it to LG England or to let my dad pick it up for me when repaired…the Customer always last!

Several months later I returned to Spain, picked up the phone from the repair center to discover that it was not working.

Without leaving the building I told them about the issue, to be told that the guarantee had expired and if I wanted to repair it I had to pay for it.

They knew that the phone was two months old when I brought it, and that for the last several months the phone had been on their premises, but they did not care, they had already taken my money, and now they could also have my phone which I smashed against one of their walls.

A bit aggressive? May be, however is not more aggressive to rob your Customers?

Needless to say that I have not bought any LG products since, and that I strongly recommend friends and peers to avoid the brand.

WHY NOT: take responsibility for defects and empathise with the Customer.

If you provide a low quality faulty product, that is followed by terrible, service do you think Customers will buy from you again?

Eroski Movil (Spain)

Frustrated with Telefonica, Lg and El Corte Ingles, and in need of a phone, I decided to buy a lovely Nokia, company who has never failed me, and to enter a contract with Eroski Movil, a new mobile company, part of one of the biggest industry, supermarket and white goods conglomerate.

I signed a year contract, and the seller guaranteed to me that there was no minimum use of the phone, his actual words were that I could use it as much or as little as I wanted, and the contract would continue even if I did not use it, as long as I paid what I used, easy as the contract was set up with a direct debit to my Spanish account.

I was so happy, it seemed too good to be true, and it was!

When I returned back to Spain to visit my family, guess what, my phone did not work, and my friends, who knew my arrival time, told me that when they called me someone else was answering.

Once I reached my parents' home I called the phone company who told me that the contract I had, even though it was sold with no minimum use, I had to make at least one call a month (or a call every two months or every three months, depending of the person in Eroski I spoke to), and as I did not, they had given my number to someone else.

Sometimes I wonder whether some companies behave the way they do due to greed, or due to pure stupidity. If the first, their business will not last long.

WHY NOT: be honest with the Customer and explain every single term to them, especially those which are likely to result in damage for the Customer.

Hackney

Hackney Council

If there are two companies in the world who deserve the award for worst Customer Service, Hackney Council (together with its sister company Hackney Homes) deserve to be at the top two.

I bought an ex-council flat in beautiful Stoke Newington (London), having Hackney Council as the freeholder.

Although I could write a full book, if not a series on how terrible, arrogant and patronising they are, I think that a few pages will suffice to illustrate why Governments and legislators should have much tougher control over some of the little kingdoms they create, i.e., local authorities.

Before moving to my new apartment, I was proactive and I wrote to Hackney informing them of my moving in date, a month in advance, as well as informing them that I would be moving alone, and hence to get the right Council Tax bill.

As I did not hear from them, I wrote to them three times, with no response until one day when I received a letter threatening me with court action if I did not pay my overdue Council tax…

How could I owe council tax, when I had not even moved in, especially considering that I had already informed them... I wrote to them again, explained, and explained, but I kept receiving threats.

I then decided to write directly to the Major, complain and start with the threating myself: I had written to them, I had already provided evidence of me paying Council tax in a different borough, why was I being threaten?

The Major, surprisingly replied, and put someone to solve the situation who then apologised and blamed IT for not having received my emails (or my letters or my calls), and it was all then sorted.

WHY: why threat your Customers, especially by assuming that they have done something wrong? Why not talk to them, why not ask and enquire to see if there is a problem, or simply some miscommunication?

Unfortunately over the years this would be a norm from Hackney employees who without exception behaved unprofessionally, threatening and were nothing but spoilt bullies as they are covered/protected by a public body, which by the way, should be taking care of people rather than harassing them.

Hackney Homes

Hackney Homes is a subsidiary company of Hackney Homes, or an Arms Lengths one, as they prefer to call it in order to get free money for the government.

Shortly after I bought the apartment, I decided it needed full redecoration and I decided to do it myself. One time while I was fitting wooden floors, someone from Hackney Homes came to the door, identified himself as the building manager and asked for the tenant.

I told him I was the owner and that there were no tenants in the apartment, to be challenged by him saying that he did not believe me, and to show him a copy of the property deeds.

When I did he complained that there was a leak from my apartment with water dropping on the wall of the building and giving me 24 hours to solve it or face court action, sweet.

Considering that I was not yet living there I found it awkward that there may be a leak, and I was not very happy to be threatened that way.

II call my plumber who confirmed that the leak was not really a leak but an overflow pipe from the water tanks on the roof, and so I told the Hackney Homes Building manager the following day when he came around to threat me again.

He went to the roof, checked, and left. I never saw him again.

WHY NOT: why not treat your Customers respectfully, given the benefit of the doubt about who they are, and most importantly, rather than start with threats and accusations, why not begin by finding the real reason of problems, and then, even if the Customer is to blame, do so politely and with respect.

British Telecom

I must say that after my experience with NTL I decided to go back to British Telecom, and continue with them forever, and in every apartment I moved into I always installed a BT line, and I never had a single fault with the line.

However, a few years ago, and after having been a Customer for many years, I once received on the mail a letter from BT offering a £50 voucher if I decided to agree to extend the contract for another 12 months.

Being a rather appealing offer, I signed the form, put it on the mail, and a few days later I received a welcome letter from BT thanking me for my decision and confirming my new contract, however no voucher was attached.

I wrote to them, emailed them, and as time was passing and I was not getting a reply, I decided to call their Customer line.

I explained to them in detail the situation, to be told that there were no trace in their records of such offer, and that they had simply continued my old contract, and that I was not entitled to any kind of voucher.

If that was not enough, I was even told that I may have dreamt of that offer because they did not ever offer something like that.

At that point I decided that perhaps it was the time to leave BT, and I asked to terminate my contract, at which point I was put through the cancellations department who were curious about my reason to cancel, which I explained in detail.

They apologised for both not having received the voucher, and second for the behaviour of the previous employee, and they asked me if I could provide a reference for the offer, which I did.

After just a few seconds, they apologised again and they offer me to send the voucher by express mail, plus credit my account with £20 for the misunderstanding, and I accepted.

WHY NOT: treat the Customer respectfully and believe what he says to start with.

WHY NOT: honour the offers, rather than trick Customers.

HOWEVER: very well done last department about apologising, finding facts, and compensating gesture for the Customer.

British Gas

Since I bought my apartment I always contracted both gas and electricity with British Gas. Not the cheapest but they had a good reputation for great service.

I never had any problem with them, like service interruption, but suddenly one day my smoke alarm went off and I saw some smoke coming out of the main electricity switchboard.

I switched the mains off, panicked, and then I called British Gas to report the fault, and get some help.

Even though the obvious urgency, I was told by British Gas, that although they were supplying me with the electricity, that area was under the control of the competitors, EDF, and I should call them, which I did, see next chapter.

WHY NOT: take responsibility and help the Customers, rather than pass the ball on, especially when you are taking their money?

EDF

Following my conversation with British Gas, please see previous chapter, I called EDF, explained the issues, all to be told that as they were not supplying me with the electricity, I should call my current supplier.

Even though I had already explained to them that I had already called my supplier and that they had asked me to call EDF, they just told me that there was nothing they could do and hung up.

They were not my suppliers, true, and they will never be.

So I decided to call National Grid.

WHY NOT: take responsibility and help the Customers, rather than pass the ball on, especially when you are taking their money?

nationalgrid

National Grid

My call to National Grid was taken in a different manner, first questions were aimed to ensure that no one was injured, and that no one would be.

Once that was cleared, I was asked to wait for one of their engineers, waiting time 30 minutes.

The engineer arrived in 10 minutes, opened the fuse box, and immediately spot the problem: he spend 2 minutes tightening 2 screws, changed a fuse, explained the reason to me, and everything for free.

WHY: why cant other companies learn from such wonderful service, attitude and well doing as National Grid provides. Sometimes is great to be a Customer!

Ryanair

If you have ever flown with Ryanair you are likely to have at least one complaint, especially if you failed to read some of the constantly changing rules aimed at making Customer paid exorbitant amounts of money for silly things.

I used to fly a lot with them (and with other airlines), not only because of the price (they are not always that cheap), but because of the convenience of some of their airport to visit small places across Europe.

In one of my trips I visited the lovely Italian city of Pisa, where I went for a long weekend. Due to fly back to London at 12.30 on a Sunday, I was in the airport my usual over two hours in advance, just a back pack with no luggage to check.

When I arrived, there were already two of Ryanair flights delayed, and soon there would be another two plus mine. So after a few hours waiting with absolutely no news from the airline or anyone, suddenly all flights were cancelled on the screen.

We all, around five or six hundred people, give or take, rushed to Ryanair's two Customer Services single desks. You can imagine, the queue, the irritation and the desperation. Obviously nor Ryanair nor its representatives gave a damn about the hundreds of passengers stranded.

People were trying to book flights for the following day, and although I was close in the queue to the desk, next day available flights were soon finished.

These days there was no wifi, or internet on the phones (well there was, but very slow and phones had small screens), or ipads, so, very limited options.

At the end I rang a friend on England who was in front of a computer with internet connection, and who booked a flight for me the following day from a different city a few hundred miles away.

Reaching that city and flying just happened because Ryanair's flight was late, otherwise a new adventure would had started.

The trip was a mess, with huge problems with Italian railways, if any German or British is reading this, please never complain about your railways until you have experienced Italian ones!

WHY NOT: inform Customers immediately if it is a delay in the flight, they deserve to know, and that gives time to react.

WHY NOT: provide facilities and help when due to your incompetence your Customers are being negatively affected.

How difficult would it be to provide a few assistants to help people book hotels, inform people, etc.

Finally, an authentic Ryanair touch, when we were all queuing to speak to a Customer Service person, several trolleys arrived with the checked baggage which was dumped in the middle of the floor, go and find yours!

How to screw your Customers – Alfredo de la Casa

Iberia

Iberia, like many other ex-country own airlines, still has a good reputation, and their staff have the attitude that they are doing you a favour for having you as a Customer, hence they keep losing money.

While other airlines have been reducing prices while improving quality, like Qatar or Emirates, Iberia keeps its already high prices, while quality has gone down hill.

I have never been much bothered about Christmas, however for my parents have always been important, so I always used to travel from London to Spain for Christmas.

As I know that prices go up steeply close to the season, I used to buy my tickets around august, yes four months ago.

And so did I one time, I paid the ticket in full to be emailed by Iberia 2 weeks before my flight to be told that my flight had been cancelled (which was not true).

I called them, and after a very long wait listening to crap music and to a pre-recorded message constantly remaining how little important Customers are for Iberia, I managed to get through someone.

After explaining the problem, I was told that my flight was overbooked so I could not flight.

Was my fault that it was overbooked, nope; did it get overbooked before I booked my seat, nope, however some criminal airlines like Iberia, do give priority to those Customers willing to pay more for a seat.

Of course if you book and pay, and you change your mind, you lose your money…

So, at the end I was given three options by lovely Iberia:

1) To fly several days later, and arrive after Christmas…what is the point?
2) To get a refund? What for, when I have booked four months ago, and prices were already outrageous while little availability.
3) To fly to Barcelona (on the other side of the country), wait four hours, and then take another flight.

At the end, as I had no good options, and because airlines have no penalties (which is why they are so rubbish) I took option three.

So I went from a 90 minute flight from London to Bilbao, to an eight hour flight experience, I may as well have flown two more hours and go to Cuba.

WHY NOT: respect the contracts and agreements with Customers.

WHY NOT: tell the truth to Customers, rather than treating them like idiots.

Iberia, part two

One year later after my first bad experience with lovely Iberia, I was again under the challenge of going back to Spain for Christmas.

With only Iberia and Easyjet flying directly to my city (and after having had a rather bad experience with the later in Switzerland) I decided to book a flight with Iberia, for my girlfriend and myself.

We both paid in full but separately, in September, and this time, it did not get cancelled, hurrah!

On the day of the flight, we both went to Heathrow airport, queued, I got my ticket, however my girlfriend at the time, of Polis nationality, was refused a boarding card, and we were asked to go to the Iberia Customer Service desk nearby, which we did.

At the so called Customer Service desk, she was asked to provide the credit card she used to buy the ticket, that she did not have as it had expired, and even though the ticket, matched the credit card name, which matched the name on her passport, which matched the name on her new credit card (with different number), and even though I used my laptop for her to log in into her bank account in front of them, for them to know that she was who she was supposed to be, Iberia refused to issue her a boarding card.

I asked to speak to the manager, who came, and told me that the only thing they could do, was to cancel her ticket, issue a refund to the original credit card and use the new credit card to re-buy her ticket.

It seemed a lot of unnecessary bureaucracy, but I asked them to go ahead. I was then told that they would refund the original £145 paid for the original ticket, and they would charge the new price, for the same seat of £575. What the hell.

Mr Iberia, Mr arrogant told me that I could take it or leave it, but if I wanted my girlfriend to fly, there were no other options.

And when you deal with a crook company, a real criminal, they know they have you against the ropes, and most people will pay the new astronomic ticket or cancel their holidays, win-win for the airline, but terrible way to start your holiday.

At that time, I was working a Business planning and risk management manager for the Department for Transport, and I was dealing, among other areas, with aviation.

So I told Mr Iberia to charge the new ticket to my credit card, which he accepted with a smile, however I told him, this time in Spanish, that the moment I landed in Bilbao I would make two calls: the first one to my credit card to cancel the charge; the second one to my director, moment in which I handled him my business card, to explain my boss the situation, and recommend that she stopped all Iberia flights to and from England due to breach of the Consumer Act and many other regulations.

He went pale, he asked me to wait, went to his office, and within a few minutes he returned with my girlfriends boarding card, no extra charge, but no apology either.

WHY NOT: honour the deal and respect it.

WHY: cheat on your Customers who are bringing you business.

WHY NOT: be decent, honest and do business the right way, according to the law, especially if you are a big multinational company.

Guess what, Iberia has been having tremendous losses, I keep hearing horror stories, I do not know many people who would fly with them, time for them to disappear.

Thai Airways

For me, and I believe for most people, holidays and relaxation go together. So aiming at having a great time on my second visit to lovely Thailand, I decided to pay more in order to fly with what they called themselves, Thai silk, although it actually was more like Thai polyester.

I booked a flight with a friend, but unfortunately he got stuck on traffic so we could not check in together. When I checked in I gave his name and ticket number to the ticket desk and I asked them if he could be seated next to me, which they agreed to.

However when he arrived, still well within the time limits to check in, his seat had been given away.

In the plain, that left later than scheduled, service was terrible. After taking off, and once the seat belt signs had gone off, I approached the flight assistants as I had observed that three seats behind my row were unoccupied.

I told them the story, I told them about the seats, but I was told that those seats were busy. Which I wonder how they could be as no one had been seating there for take off and it was a direct flight.

Later on I observed that there were no passengers occupying such seats, but that the crew were using them for themselves to sleep.

Dinner time arrived, and with just two options for food available, I was shocked that only the vegetarian option was left, with no other choice.

The flight was full of entertainment, and I do not mean the tvs, which were not working but more about a fight between Arabs, and then to see next to me how the toilet was used as an emergency room, and get the typical call from the pilot, "is there a doctor on board", when we were flying over Iraq, please do not make an emergency landing here!

Happy to land in Bangkok, when my new luggage finally arrived, I found that it was broken.

My next stop was the lost luggage desk, who took several photos of my luggage, made many notes, and after over an hour waiting I was given a list of addresses in Thailand where I was told to take my suitcase for repair.

I was fuming: so they break my suitcase due to carelessness, they waste one hour of my time, and then they expect me to spend the first day of my holidays in a foreign country traveling around to have my suitcase repaired? No way! Thai silk, my as**!

The return flight was equally disastrous, and like with Iberia, I will fly with Thai Airways never again.

WHY NOT: honour what you agree with Customers, and if you have two people traveling together and seats are available, allocate them properly; and if you don't want to do so, don't promise!

WHY NOT: have enough meals of the most likely meal to be ordered. Which percentage of the population flying from London is likely to be vegetarian? Do you ever think?

WHY NOT: inform passengers if there is an issue, no matter how minor, on board, especially when they can see something happening, and panic is not good.

WHY NOT: take responsibility if you screw it up, like breaking your Customer's property, do you really think that it is fair that you break someone luggage and you ask them to solve the problem, rather than either solving it yourself, of buying new one on the spot?

Insure and Go

On my trip back from Thailand I contacted Insure and Go, with who I had contracted a comprehensive travel and health insurance, in order to request compensation for my broken suitcase.

I rang them, explained the situation and they asked me for a long list of documents (tickets, ticket reservations, report from the airline,… you name it).

I prepared and sent to them absolutely everything by registered mail, and one month later I received a letter from them, saying that even though I had no excess in my policy, because the original cost of my suitcase was very small, they would not give me any money due to the low value of my loss…

I was speechless: so rather than as a company be happy that they have to pay little, they refuse on the basis of the cost being low… of course because then they pay nothing.

WHY NOT: honour your part of the contract.

WHY: make up new, silly stupid, rules. And

WHY: bother your Customers with preparing lots of documentation if you already know the value of the item and you do not plan to pay.

The answer, I guess, is that rogue companies here abuse, hoping that Customers will not take them to Court, and that most Customers will not keep all the un-necessary papers. Ombudsman, where are you?

American Express Travel Insurance

After the Insurance and Go fiasco I decided to shop around the market, and I then realised that American Express, one of my favourite companies, was also offering the service.

I bought one of their policies, and I kept renewing it year after year.

One time, one of my suitcases got broken, the airline, Ryanair, refused any compensation so I made an insurance claim.

I called the help desk, explained the situation and I was asked for the date of the trip, airline, flight number, and brand, cost and age of the suitcase.

As my suitcase was 5 years old, the agent apologised for having to tell me that, only a percentage of the original value would be covered. I was expecting the worse, but they just deducted 20% for wear and tear.

He then asked whether I agreed with his estimate which I did. Asked me to deliver some documents to him, and he told me that I would receive compensation within 7 working days, which arrived in just three.

What a great experience, fair, fast and uncomplicated.

WHY: companies can not learn from such simple, but great ways to operate like this. It is simple, straight forward and fair for everyone, and most important, keeps Customers loyal!

Axa Insurance

Although my freeholder took care of the buildings insurance (at my expense), I still needed contents insurance, so after studying several quotes I signed with Axa Insurance.

I never filed a claim, and I kept renewing year after year, until one year when, I received a renewal letter with a huge price increase.

One week later I rang AXA, to complain about the steep price increases, which were not fair, as I had never made a claim, and in fact they should be reducing my insurance price rather than increasing it.

When I spoke to the Customer Service representative, he asked me for the Customer number, and he told me that prices were like that, to take it or leave it.

While I was still thinking, he told me that he just realised that the offer has expired the day before, and that if I wanted to renew at that time, the new cost would be 15% more.

I was shocked and quite angry. I asked him, how could the price of a service like insurance, where the key items are the characteristics of my apartment suffer a 15% increase in less than 24 hours.

His answer was outrageous: he did not know and he did not care, if I did not like the new price I could go to a different company. Guess what, I did.

WHY NOT: be fair, and rather than be greedy and expect your Customers to cover your expenses due to poor management, take responsibility for your own deeds.

WHY NOT: use logic and respect your Customers. Was it really necessary to increase the insurance fee 15% on top of the 10% already increased just because I was one day late in accepting?

HSBC Insurance

After my experience with Axa, I needed a new contents insurance for my apartment, and I came across HSBC Home insurance.

I requested a quote, and to my surprise, not only the quote came quite fast, but it was much cheaper than Axa, more comprehensive, and lower excess.

I have never made a claim in the last 5 years, however I must say that HSBC has not put the prices up, which is fair, because the risks have not changed.

I have no intention to change, even if I find cheaper insurance; plus I have recommended HSBC insurance to many friends who are equally happy.

WHY: when you are doing something well, and make money with it, not keep doing it (or even improving it). AXA learn!

Rodizio Rico

Rodizio Rico is a Brazilian restaurant, so popular that has now become a chain.

After having visited and enjoyed it a few times, I decided to take a group of my friends to enjoy it together.

So there we arrived 12 of us, ready to have a wonderful Friday night dinner. We ordered a couple of bottles of wine to start with, but unfortunately one of them was corked.

We called the waiter, told him that the bottle was corked and we asked for a new one. Without even checking, he told us that the wine was fine, and that because the bottle had already been opened it was our fault if we did not like the wine but we still had to pay for it.

We asked for the manager who told us the same thing to which he added that it was obvious that we did not know about wine, and perhaps in the future we should stick to beer. Interesting considering that in the group three of us were in the wine business, and there was even a sommelier with us.

At this point we told him that the wine was faulty not us or our knowledge, and that we would not pay for it, what is more that we would not have dinner there anymore, and that he had two options: either we finished the other bottle of wine and pay for it, or leave immediately without paying anything, or he could always call the police.

At the end we paid for the good bottle, drunk it, a left. Well done staff and manager for kicking out 12 Customers from an almost empty restaurant and not seeing them ever again.

WHY NOT: check if the Customer is right when he/she complains?

Why not give Customers the benefit of the doubt, and why insult Customers? All unnecessary never leading to anything good.

Wetherspoons Birmingham Airport

I have visited Birmingham many times, almost every time for business. One of these times I attended a conference with my colleagues in a posh hotel, however we were not too keen on the food offered there, so we decided to go to the nearby pub, Wetherspoons, at the Airport.

We arrived 10 minutes before 9 in the evening, no Customers there, and once we had chosen a table big enough for the 15 of us, two us took the menus to decide what to order.

Within minutes, the manager, not looking much older than 23, came and violently grabbed the menus from our hands (moment he deserved to be punch on the nose for how violent he was), and he started screaming to us that they were not taking orders after 9pm and that we should go.

I checked my watch, in fact all of us did, and we pointed to him that it was still 10 to 9, so we officially were on time to order.

He then told us in a rather rude way to leave, and so we did. Birmingham may not be the culinary capital of the word, but you can always find a bite to eat, and we did.

On my return to London I wrote to Wetherspoons complaining, first as a Customer, second as a shareholder. I never received a reply.

WHY: why kick out Customers, especially if they are on time? Why drive business away, especially considering that there were not doing much business at the time, rather than be grateful for having extra income.

WHY NOT: answer correspondence from your Customers, not to mention you shareholders, they take the time to give you vital information to improve, and you ignore it rather than being grateful?

MORRISONS

Morrisons supermarkets

Morrisons is one of the big supermarket chains that, as oligopoly, dominates a good part of the British supermarket scene.

I used to do my shopping with them, mostly due to proximity to my apartment, however it came a time, probably following some management change, that every single time I shopped there I was overcharged in the bill, so I decided to be careful.

I decided to make sure I memorised the prices, and roughly added up the total of the items I was buying before paying, and this way I realised that it was common practice in Morrisons to put one price on the shelves, and one much higher price at the cashier.

So next time I shopped there, I noticed their trick, so after telling the cashier, who asked me to go to refunds. The employees in charge of refunds, went and checked and asked me to fill a form so that I could get a refund or allow me to return the product.

This was common for them, as frequently their practice was to shelve a product under the price of a much lowered priced items of the same brand.

Several times I spoke to the manager about this, and his reply varied from asking me to be more careful when checking to blaming Customers who moved products around: of course Customers go and move piles of products around!

I reported them to the local authorities, and I believe an investigation took place, and I stopped shopping there.

WHY NOT: be honest and charge what you advertise rather than trick your Customers. People are not stupid, and they do not like to be robbed!

Santander

After successfully banking with Abbey National for many years, when Santander bought them, I stayed with them, and when the time arrived for me to have a mortgage they offered what I wanted, and I went for an offset mortgage.

An offset mortgage has a savings account linked to it, which means that you can save at the same rate that you are being charged.

The first trick, although probably legal, that Santander had for mortgages, was different mortgage fees, ranging from a few hundred to almost a thousand pounds.

The mortgage fee, which in theory is to pay for the costs of doing the mortgage paperwork, should be free, as the bank is already making money, good money, from the interest it charges.

However if we accept that a fee should be paid, it should be the same regardless the one you chose, because all of them have the same amount of paperwork.

Who would go for an expensive fee when you can go for much cheaper ones? I guess idiots like me, who have a degree in Economics and are qualified Chartered Accountants, because we tend to read and I realised that the interest rates associated with the different fees were rather different.

But most people who do not understand finance and accountancy terms, would have gone for a small fee, and ending up paying thousands and thousands of pounds more over the life of the mortgage.

WHY NOT: be clear with your Customers and try to explain, in simple terms, all the options and the implications of them, rather than tricking them. This is so wrong…

Santander, mortgages part 2

Another benefit of the offset mortgage is that you can change the size of your payments to adapt to your financial circumstances.

As I was doing well, several times I rang Santander asking them to transfer some money from my offset savings account to reduce the mortgage.

Every single time the person I spoke to tried to convince me that I was doing the wrong thing, and that I should keep the money on savings rather than paying my mortgage in advance.

Every single time I had to battle to get what I, the Customer, wanted. Usually the conversation ended by telling them that I was a Chartered Accountant, and that if they continued to refuse my instructions I would have to report them to the Banking Ombudsman.

Terrible Customer I am!

For those of you not finance educated: the bigger the mortgage base the bigger the interest you pay, and because mortgages' interest rates are not lineal but gradual (at the beginning most of your repayments are interest rather than loan repayment) the sooner you reduce the principal, the more your interest payments reduce.

WHY NOT: be clear with your Customers and try to explain, in simple terms, all the options and the implications of them, rather than tricking them.

Especially when the Customer is requesting the most beneficial option for him, why try to convince him to do something that will result in the Customer being worse off?

MBNA cards

MBNA is one of the biggest issuers of credit cards, which they do under many different brands.

I used to hold two of their cards, and like with any other credit cards that I subscribe, the first thing I always do is to set up an automatic direct debit to pay for all expenses in full, so that I do not incur any interest. As I never spend money that I don't have, with the exception of the mortgage, this gives me peace of mind.

So I was very surprised when suddenly I received a letter from MBNA informing me of an exorbitant interest fee for the credit in my delayed payments of my credit card. What?

I rang them immediately and I was told that because I had not paid my last statement, I had incurred interest and fees that now I was liable for.

I told them that how could that be possible considering that I had a direct debit with them and funds in my bank, not to mention an overdraft facility.

They checked and I was told that the direct debit was no longer active and therefore the money had not been taken from my account so I had to pay for everything.

When I asked who had cancelled the direct debit, because I had not, they told me they did not know, but that I had to pay.

Threatening letters followed from their side. After I checked with my bank, who told me that they never cancelled direct debits without an order from their Customers, I paid by transfer the amount of my purchases and I cancelled my credit card. One Customer lost.

Threats kept coming until I wrote to them again, this time threatening them myself with legal action and with reporting them to the financial commission for fraud. Letters stopped.

WHY: always blame the Customer, who is who brings money to companies, rather than investigating and taking ownerships of their own mistakes.

1and1

I used to register many domains with 1and1, sometimes hoping for new future companies, some other times just when a good name crossed my mind.

So after the usual two year registration period/contract if domains were not renewed they would expire.

However 1and1 decided to automatically renew them, which is illegal, and make it almost impossible for Customers to cancel the renewal.

One of these times, one of my domains that I no longer wanted was auto-renewed and my credit card charged. I contested the charge but I did not get anything but an automated reply from 1 and 1.

When I tried to cancel another domain hat I did not want, their process was so cumbersome that I could not manage to do so.

So after several calls and emails, with no success I was left with no option than cancel my credit card, so that 1and1 could no longer charge me; and to threat them with court action, as by auto renewing domains, or in other words, by selling me their products without my permission or desire, they were seriously violating the Sales of Goods Act.

This seemed to work, as someone from 1and1 contacted me and we came into an agreement.

WHY NOT: respect your Customers' wishes, why break the law, and why force Customers to pay for products that they do not want, and which they have not asked to buy?

Foreign and Commonwealth Office

Long time ago I applied for a post at the FCO, which was offered only to University graduates.

I filled the application form, I sent it, however after a few weeks I received a call from their Human Resources department telling me that they had to refuse my application because I could not prove that I was a university graduate.

Even though I had provided a CV, a copy of my degree and even a stamped document from the university confirming that I had graduated several years ago, their reply was that as they could not find my university in the book they had listing universities, it was obvious that my university did not exist. What the…

With all my respects to the FCO, how can you employ in HR someone so thick? Especially considering that my first degree, my only degree at the time, is from a public university of Spain, actually one with the best reputation?

WHY NOT: listen to your Customer and do some research, rather than assume that the Customer is lying?

Stanstead Express

I used to be a frequent user of Stanstead Express train taking you from Liverpool Street and from Tottenham Hale to Stanstead Airport in 45 minutes. Expensive, actually very expensive (sometimes more than the flight) but fast.

In a couple of occasions I booked a return ticket, and when I tried to use the second trip leg, I was shocked that the train company had decided not to stop on my station.

Later on, when working for the Department for Transport, I discovered the financial reasons behind such decisions, however from the Customer Service point of view, awful.

I contacted them, and because I had to go to the center of London rather than my stop, I missed my last tube back home, so I had to take a taxi.

In both occasions they refused to pay my taxi fare.

WHY: not honour your part of the contract, when you expect Customers to honour theirs, especially considering that in the UK if you are found to be traveling without a valid ticket you commit a crime and could easily end with a criminal record. Unfair that the strict law seems to be applied to only on side.

London Buses

For the last few years if you travel in London Buses, part of Transport for London, you may get lucky, find little traffic and have a swift trip until suddenly the bus driver will stop in the bus stop and refuse to leave. A few minutes later he will play a pre-recorded message saying that the bus is on hold "in order to regulate the service".

In other words, it means that for once that rather than having a slow delayed service, the bus is going even quicker than expected, rather than enjoy and get compensated for the large amount of times that buses are seriously delayed, they delay the bus so that there are no more bus "runs" than scheduled.

The reason behind this is purely financial: since the bus services are run by private companies, they are being paid per trip rather than by shift, which means that in a bad day they get paid the same even if they run less services than scheduled; however in a good day they will either reduce the speed or have to be paid for the extra runs.

Rather than providing the better service, at a cost, they choose to slow down the trips, even though if further down the route it may get bad, and end up overall delayed.

WHY NOT: provide excellent service when possible, especially considering the absurd high costs that passengers have to pay when traveling using public transport in London, and especially considering that when the service is substandard (which is most of the times), you still charge the same to passengers. Unfair!

AOL (UK)

I have been an AOL Customer for over two decades, and overall I have been quite satisfied with them.

I am still a Customer, my main email address is AOL, and I use them as my internet service provider (ISP) in my apartment in London. They are not cheap, but service is decent.

However a few years back, one day out of the blue there was no internet. Being a bit of a techy myself I checked the obvious things: turn on and off the router, change the filter, tried different computers but no service.

So I decided to call them, and report the fault. After the usual terrible automated system, I managed to speak to a person. Who asked me to do a series of steps that I had already done.

Even though I told her that I have already checked it, she insisted that I checked it again. She then told me that everything seemed ok on her side, so I may have a virus on my computer; not according to my antivirus, and definitely not in every compute I had!

So she told me that she would investigate and call me within an hour, which is what unprofessional employees say hoping that the problems get solved by itself, which never does. If not, the Customer can always call again, which I did.

I had to go the same steps once more, this time the operator asked me to wait on the line while he checked with BT about the status of the nearby main switch, with ended up being the reason for the problem.

WHY NOT: do your job and investigate faults, rather than expect them to get solved by themselves, and rather than blaming the Customer (or in this case, my computers) try to find and solve the reason for the fault.

AOL part 2

Just a few months ago my tenant, now living in my London apartment, called me as she had been with no internet for five days

She called AOL, who asked her to follow the usual steps, and then AOL asked her to agree to send an engineer a week later, a week!

Who can nowadays survive without internet for a week?

When the engineer arrived he immediately found the fault: because AOL had upgraded their systems, the modem was too old (3 years old!) and needed to be replaced.

AOL offered to send a new modem but it would take two weeks. Auch!

WHY NOT: consider your Customers and the effect on them when considering major changes.

And if you go ahead with changes why not inform your Customers in advance, so they know what to expect.

And one week to send an engineer? Why not a month or a year!

Samsung

After many years of loyalty to Nokia, and after seeing that at the time even their latest phones were outdated, I decided to buy what is was widely considered, with the Iphone, the best smartphone of the market: Samsung Galaxy

I soon had problems with the usb connection as my computer, or any other computer, would not recognise it any more.

After doing some research on the internet I discovered that this was actually a fault of the phone, that Samsung had not yet managed nor to officially recognise nor to solve.

I was then about to relocate to Vietnam, so I needed an unlocked phone, so I spoke to my mobile provider who agreed to unlock my phone, as long as I paid the rest of my two year contract, which I did.

However they failed to unlock it, so they sent me to Samsung Service Center where I personally brought the pone.

After waiting for an engineer he came, took my phone, disappeared for 20 minutes and returned with my phone which was given to the receptionist and then to me.

The receptionist told me that the phone could not be unlocked because they could not use the usb port which was damaged, and because my phone was 14 months old, it was no longer under guarantee.

If that was not bad enough, the engineer had completely deleted everything on my phone from contacts to applications. When I complaint, his response was that he had not done anything or deleted anything. Great.

Needless to say that I will not ever buy any Samsung phone or tablet.

And now that I am in the process of moving to a new apartment where I am buying all electronics and white goods, and where Samsung is considered a good brand, I have just bought a vacuum cleaner from them, and this just because it was the only option available

WHY NOT: recognise the faults and solve them, rather than ignore them, blame the Customers, or simply avoid responsibilities based on guarantee times. Ok they sold me a phone they took my money, never again. I am finding many people with the same experience with

Samsung, I am still to meet one unhappy Iphone Customer!

PC World

Last year I went back to London on holidays and to visit friends, a wonderful opportunity to do some shopping.

As my laptop was somehow showing its age, I decided to buy a brand new Toshiba laptop from PC World, one of the very few retailers who still has a shop in the high street. Part of their promotion was that they would install the Operative System for you, nice!

So I went I bought the laptop, and when I mentioned to them about the OS installation I realised that they had forgotten to mention in their "offer" that they charged £100 to do so…really? £100 to insert 2-3 dvds and let the clock continue?

I installed the OS myself. The following month I was shocked to have an unexpected charge on my Amex card, £20 from PC world. Charge that would repeat every single month until I finally managed to convince Amex to put a stop on them.

PC World had decided to charge me £20 a month for extended guarantee providing UK home service, they even claimed that I requested it when Amex approached them.

Thanks god that Amex employs people with a brain, who found a bit odd that I, living in Vietnam, would request a UK extended guarantee…

WHY NOT: honour the part of the deal without hidden charges. Why try to impose unrequested guarantees and services on your Customers, knowing that many will not be bothered to cancel, this is nothing but fraud!

The Vietnam Times (but also suffering the wrong doing of Western companies)

Gammer Restaurant

Gammer is a rather popular Eastern European restaurant n HCMC, it has its own brewery, it is huge and offers a large selection of both Vietnamese and Eastern European food.

So when two of my friends were visiting Vietnam for the first time, and as they had already had enough Vietnamese food we decided to take them to this place which is local and popular.

The place was almost empty, we were suggested a table that we accepted. We then ordered some beers, and some food, but several minutes later the manager came and asked us to move to another table.

When I asked him why, considering that drinks had already been served, that we were waiting for food, and especially that the floor was almost empty, he told me that some VIP guest had just arrived and wanted that table so we had to move.

My initial feeling was to move, not table but out, but I was convinced not to by my f riends. Mistake.

We ordered a selection of food, including grilled prawns, and at some point food started to arrive. About three or four times we reminded the waitress about the prawns, to be told yes, yes yes, but it was no, no no.

So about 90 minutes after having ordered the prawns, and with our meal almost finished we called the waitress, asked her to cancel the prawns and bring the bill.

She automatically went to the kitchen and returned to tell us that the prawns would be served in 5 minutes, (same as she had told us before), but we insisted to get the prawn dish cancelled.

A few minutes later and when we were getting ready to go for a city tour, and the prawns arrived. We asked her to take them back but she refused.

Then the argument started, first between the waitress and my girlfriend and then between the manager and my girlfriend, all sort of excuses and arguments were given by the staff: from take the prawns and eat them at you home tonight (of yes, let's walk around in the heat for a few hours with a box of prawns), to "we already told you that it would take long to grill the prawns" (which was not true), to that it was our mistake and we had to pay for them.

If you are thinking that there may be some issues due to language barrier, don't, as my girlfriend (now my wife) is Vietnamese and was doing most of the talking.

At the end I had to stand up and give the manager three options: to take the prawns off the bill, to call the police or let us go without paying. After more arguing and 15 minutes later the bill arrived, with no prawns charged to it.

That evening I wrote a letter of complaint to the restaurant management. Three weeks later they replied saying "sorry you had bad experience in our restaurant, we hope next time you come will be better for you".

WHY NOT: admit mistakes? And in particular if you make them, make sure to correct them. Whether the waitress forgot to order the prawns to the kitchen (four times!) or whether it was the kitchen who forgot, live with it, if the Customer asks you to cancel a dish, especially one which is 90 minutes late, and that you have probably not even started cooking, learn from it.

WHY blame the Customer, why lie, and why accuse and pass the blame to the Customer? If you make a mistake, start by apologising, and try to correct it and learn from it.

WHY NOT use valuable feedback. Companies should reward Customers who take the time to complain, as they are giving them free great feedback about their

products and services. Wishing them good luck next time, is like telling them to f*** off, and they will!

Vietcombank

When I arrived to Vietnam I was taken to Vietcombank by my HR Manager, as according to her it was the best bank in Vietnam.

After signing endless forms, signing more times than any minister does on a week, I had my bank account open, and even internet access to it.

One week later I found an apartment to rent, and after a month I decided to transfer the rent via online transfer. All fine, my money left the account, and I even received a transaction reference.

A week later I received a call from the real estate agency as my landlord was very angry because I had not paid the rent. I told the agency about my transfer who then told the landlord who then come to see me, quite angry until I presented to him the transaction that luckily I had printed out.

He then called his bank, and came back to me as there was no trace of the money. So I dedicated my next day's lunch hour to go to my local Vietcombank.

I explained the situation to them and they told me that everything was ok and the money had been paid, so after arguing for a while, I decided to call my landlord and pass the phone to the Vietcombank's employee, for them to argue with each other.

After 15 minutes, while I waited patiently, the employee told me that because I had made a mistake, they could not find the destination account and therefore it was my fault that the money (that fifteen minutes before had been confirmed as transferred by him), had not been transferred.

My obvious next question was, where is the money then as it had not been refunded to my account, he told me that because they did not know what to do with it, they were keeping it and that they were waiting for me to go to the branch and tell them what to do with the money…I give you may word, this is a true story.

I left and the following day I opened a new account with a new bank, and I then went to Vietcombank to close my account.

I was then told that I could not close my account there, but that I had to go to the main branch and present to them certified copies of my passport, visa,… I decided not to close my account but I took almost all my money out.

WHY NOT call the Customer immediately if you have a problem with a money transfer.

WHY blame the Customer, when it is obvious that all the details are correct

WHY not let someone close their own account, or make it so difficult, just to keep a large number of unused accounts open, and show that you have so many (fictional) Customers?

TECHCOMBANK

Techcombank

After the trouble at Vietcombank, Techcombank was a delight, with staff that could actually speak English, all fantastic until one day I received a message from Techombank on my mobile, giving me my username, access code and pin to use my mobile to access my bank account.

I could not believe that someone would be so stupid, not to mention unprofessional, to send by such unsecure means absolutely everything needed to access (and empty) my bank account.

So I jumped on my motorbike and drove to the closest branch of Techcombank. I had to talk to three different people, and then I finally was met by the branch Director, who told me that I should not complain and that I should even be happy that the bank was giving the mobile service for free!

I gave up trying to get him to see the obvious security risks, so I told him to cancel the service, which he refused. I then told him that if he did not and I ever received one single message with access codes to my bank account, I would go to the press and make sure that everyone knew that it was not safe to keep money in Techcombank, to which he agreed to cancel the service.

I am not entirely sure that he actually cancelled the service, but I have not received a text message from the bank, of any kind, since!

I will not even start with the security implications of their actions, however:

WHY NOT check with Customers first before imposing a new service (or product) which they had not requested.

WHY not follow the Customer's desire to cancel a service, especially considering that the Customer did not request it.

SONY

Sony

Although I have always loved the design and specifications of Sony products, I have tended to find them overpriced when comparing to competition.

I was (still am) a frequent user of mp3 players, so after several poor experiences with low and medium cost ones, I decided to buy the latest Sony mp3 player.

With 16 GB internal memory and almost 40 hours of battery life, it really sounded like being well worth the extra price.

I bought one from Amazon who was delivered quite fast. Unfortunately the 40 hours battery were more like 12, and after several weeks waiting for the battery to grow I decided to return it to Amazon (see next chapter), with who agreed for a replacement.

I was happy with the replacement for a couple of years (even though the battery was still far from reaching half of the advertised hours) until one day that I tried to switch it on, the light came for a split second and nothing happened.

I took it to Sony's technical service who after four days called me back to tell me that the mother board had died and I needed to replace it, at a cost higher than a new mp3 player.

WHY NOT make products of such quality that justifies the high price.

WHY NOT make repairs at reasonable prices, rather than charge more for a replacement than for a new one.

How to screw your Customers – Alfredo de la Casa

Amazon (UK)

Although I have always loved the design and specifications of Sony products, I have tended to find them overpriced when comparing to competition.

I was (still am) a frequent user of mp3 players, so after several poor experiences with low and medium cost ones, I decided to buy the latest Sony mp3 player.

With 16 GB internal memory and almost 40 hours of battery life, it really sounded like being well worth the extra price.

I bought one from Amazon who was delivered quite fast. Unfortunately the 40 hours battery were more like 12, and after several weeks waiting for the battery to grow I decided to return it to Amazon (see next chapter), with who agreed for a replacement.

No questions asked, and very supportive after sales team. Within three days the replacement arrived.

What a fantastic Customer service, understanding and professional team! Needless to say that I have been a loyal Customer to Amazon even since.

WHY NOT: learn from companies, that although young, exceed in understanding Customers and serving them.

How to screw your Customers – Alfredo de la Casa

SONY

Sony, part 2

Following the pressure of my wife, who was then working for Sony, and after having enjoyed a Sony camera without faults (at least until it was stolen), I was convinced to buy a Sony tablet.

As usual more expensive than the competitors with similar characteristics, I was happy with until just 12 months after having bought it, it decided to stop connecting to any wifi network.

I did some search on the internet, and it seemed a problem common to several Sony tablets and phones. So once more I decided to take it to Sony technical support, and for the second time with a Sony product, I was told that the mother board, costing several hundred dollars, needed to be replaced. It was days since my 12 month guarantee had expired and I was fuming, I still am!

I now own just a new mp3 player and a phone from Sony, both presents from my wife (she loves Sony even though she left the company over a year ago), and a brand new Sony Bravia TV, again my wife's decision. But as you can imagine, I will not buy any more Sony products, unless I am forced to!

The terrible combination of high price and low quality, is probably one of the many reasons why Sony, once a top quality top technology company, seems to be now on the verge of bankruptcy, following several years of astronomic losses.

WHY NOT make product of such quality that justifies the high price.

WHY NOT make repairs at reasonable prices, rather than charge more for a replacement than for a new one.

Hai Long 5 Hotel (HCMC)

Having visited over 30 countries, this hotel chain is the worst I have ever experienced, in particular Hai Long 5 in Hai Ba Trung.

This chain represents everything what Vietnam should get rid of: overpriced, miss sold description of rooms, bellboys going the extra mile to get any business out of you, including prostitution, rooms with no water, or hot water only,…

In this hotel rooms which are advertised with window, for which you pay extra, do usually have a window, however they are looking at the hall, not the street or even the backyard. Beds full of bugs, noisy,… a very long list of things you don't want to experience when you are actually looking to relax and have a good time and experience.

I visited this hotel when on holidays before moving to Vietnam. Being advertised as three stars, it does not deserve even one!

I was staying with a friend, and after a long flight from Europe we arrived to Ho Chi Minh City. After checking in and agreeing with my friend to meet in reception in 30 minutes, I was surprised that when I came down he was already there, complaining in reception because he had no water in the room; the manager ensured him that it would have water in one hour.

We went out to explore the city, and when we came back several hours later, my friend did indeed have water in his bath, but only hot scalding water!

He ended up using my bathroom to shower and making another complain. We went out again and when we returned we found someone in my friend's room who had virtually unassembled his full bathroom, so we left again. When we came back again, things seemed to be finally sorted.

The night was interesting, this time it was my turn to suffer the "quality" of Hai Long hotels, as when I went to bed, suddenly I started to feel something biting me everywhere, so I switched the lights on to see the bed sheets were full of small bugs.

I rang reception who told me that they would solve it the following day, they didn't, thanks god I had a strong insect repellent, but not a very nice companion to sleep with or to care for my skin either.

The second night was equally "fascinating" especially when suddenly one of the bell boys, came in the middle of the night, opened my door without even knocking, and went directly to the bathroom to see what was happening as the room downstairs had a leak.

I could go on with my first hotel experience in Vietnam, but I think you can get the picture. And this is a hotel in the expensive area of town!

WHY NOT check that basic things like water and clean sheets are available, on a daily basis, but especially when having new guests?

WHY NOT knock on someone doors and wait for him/her to open before entering, it is basic education, isn't it?

G2000 (Vietnam)

G2000 is one of the largest manufacturers and retailers of clothing in Vietnam. With their own factories and many shops, including outlets on the luxury shopping centers, it has gained a very good reputation for quality.

On my arrival to Vietnam, I decided to expand my wardrobe as it was limited due to plane luggage restrictions. So I visited one of the shops next to the University I was teaching at, and I identified several nice looking, good feel, a bit expensive, but nice shirts.

When I had decided for the models I wanted to buy, I asked for my size and then to try them, but I was told that they did not have a changing room, but not to worry because their sizes were made to international standards, and in any case I could always return them within a week.

I took them home and open them for washing before wearing, and I tried one just to be on the safe side, and the shirt was too small, way too small.

I have worn size 43 (size 9 in the UK) for the last 20 years or so, and until this time I never had to try the shirts as they always fit me as long as they were size 43.

So the following day I took them to the same shop I bought them from, same sales assistant, who immediately told me that as I had opened the packages I could not return them, and they could nor change them nor refund.

It did not matter how much I insisted on the promises made by the assistant the day before, I fail to get a bigger size (that then I discover they did not make) or to get my money back.

Unfortunately I have learn the hard way that in Vietnam, most sellers have been "educated" to sell whatever the result is, and to never give the money back.

For example last weekend I had a rather big argument in a shop because they insisted that the belt they wanted to sell to me did fit me if I hold my breath a bit… it was obvious that I would not be able to hold my breath forever so that their biggest size belt fits and I buy it from them, but their target was to get my money then and there.

WHY lie to the Customer, by first using different size standards (saving just a few cms of material), then guaranteeing the standards as international, ensuring that I can return within one week but then refusing to accept the return. Yes, they got my money that day but never again, not to mention the large amount of people that I have convinced not to buy from them. In the long term they lose rather than win!

Coopmart (Vietnam)

Coopmart is the biggest chain of "modern" supermarkets in Vietnam, very popular due to its size and convenience.

I joined their loyalty programme, and as a result of my shopping I was awarded a 100.000 VND voucher (roughly $5). I put it in my pocket and I started my shopping trip.

The air con must have been broken because it was extremely hot and humid, so by the time I reached the till 20 minutes after, I noticed that the voucher, printed in very thin paper, which I had put on my shirt pocket, was partly broken. Nothing missing just when I tried to take it out I teared one third on the middle.

When I tried to use it, the cashier refused to accept it because it was broken. It did not matter that I showed her that it had been issued, dated and stamped less than 30 minutes before, she then asked me to go to the top floor to take it to the Chief Accountant, who refused to accept it, because she suspected fraud… I was speechless.

I left the voucher with her and the shopping with the cashier, and I have not visited the supermarket in the last 6 months.

I know that due to the oligopolistic situation of supermarkets in Vietnam is a matter of time before I have to return, but so far I have gone from shopping twice or three times a week to none, I hope the top cheese at Coopmart find it out and reward the efficient accountant, surely neither will happen!

WHY not trust your Customers unless they give you a real reason not to. Was it my fault that the voucher was broken, you could say I was sloppy and the mix of me being fat, weather hot, no aircon and the razor thin paper used to make it resulted in it getting easily broken.

However the vouchers are numbered and coded, they make you sign in a book when they give it to you, so it was not difficult to check that first, that voucher was real, and second that no one had used it, but why help and serve the Customer? And more important why accuse the Customer of fraud, especially if innocent.

JARVIS
Investment Management plc

X-O (Jarvis Investments) UK

Several years back I opened two trading accounts with X-O a branch of Jarvis Investments in the UK.

They offer(ed) one of the many simple easy to use platforms to invest in shares, ISAs, etc, and I have been with them several years without trouble.

Early this week they sent me an email saying that they would soon change their trading platform but that I should do nothing yet, and this very morning (Saturday) they sent me another email saying that they have rolled over the new system, that I can no longer access my account or the trading platform, and that in order to access the new platform I need to activate the new account, link provided, for which I will need my email address, date of birth and address.

I have never understood why stupid companies do not ever think about the Customer before making stupid decisions, or why do not even bother to put themselves in the Customers' shoes or simply ask a few Customers for feedback before going ahead.

If I already registered in the past (twice as I have two accounts with them), why not simply transfer the data from one system to another which can be done almost costless and smoothly, rather than ask thousands of people to do it individually.

So I started my Saturday by going to the activation page, where I was not asked for my address or date of birth but I was asked for my account number, a number that was never used by X-O to make transactions.

Did X-O bothered to send the account number with their email, of course not. Have they bothered to provide an option to retrieve it, of course not.

Fortunately I had a record of my account number, I followed the steps but nothing happened. I still cannot log in or access my account. I have already emailed them, let's see how fast and how useful and helpful their reply is.

WHY NOT think about your Customer first? Try to put yourself in your Customers' shoes and see how changes that you impose on them my affect them.

WHY NOT spend some time thinking about what can go wrong, what Customers may need, and provide it straight away and before hand.

Maximark (Vietnam)

Maximark, another of the big supermarket chains present in Vietnam, has just a few hypermarkets around, they are big, dark and not close to the city center, but they tend to have a good selection of spirits and foreign food, which appeals to me.

I go there once every two to three months, make a very big order that lasst me for a while. The last time I went, both my wife and I were approached by security as we entered the supermarket, and quite rudely we were told to leave, scorted out and asked to deposit our bags (normal handbag for my wife, and small should bad with my tablet for me) with security.

I refused to do so and the two security guards told me that then I could not enter the supermarket because I was obviously going there to rob, nice.

So I left and I asked to see a supervisor, who in different words told me the same.

As I told him, if they do not trust me, the Customer, with all their security in place, why should I trust my valuables to them, especially considering that there have been many reported cases when valuables are stolen from the consigns at supermarkets. No reply, we left, probably forever.

WHY NOT trust your Customers rather than assume that they are there to steal from you.

How many people are likely to buy or do business with someone who without reason already suspects them to be criminals, I will not, and not many people will.

Would not be easier to respect your Customers, to expect them not to steal, as I am sure is the case with 99% of them, and if needed increase the number of cameras, security personnel, or simply ask to show their bags at the end of the shopping experience.

How to screw your Customers – Alfredo de la Casa

Big C

Big C is the second largest supermarket retailer in Vietnam. Part of the Casino Group (France) they have been here for a while and they have been trying to build a reputation about the freshness and quality of their products, trying to convince middle income locals to buy from them rather than from the street wet markets.

I have been buying from them for a while with no major issues, they have a good selection of products, prices are reasonable and you can (usually) pay by credit card.

I have however had two relatively small issues with Big C, which also known by the expats as the Big Con (and another similar appellation ending in unt).

The first one was when some genius buyer decided to change the supplier of plastic bags, obviously for a cheaper alternative, but also thinner like air, so a few meters after having left the cashier, one of my bags, packed by her, just broke and my shopping ended noisily on the floor as two gherkin jars broke on the floor.

No one of the almost 50 staff around me did anything apart from look at me. Since then I always double or treble bag everything I buy there, so unless the genius who decided to change the bag supplier buys the bags half or on third cheaper, he is actually losing money, especially considering that a lot of Customers do as I do.

The second issue, much more serious, happened last weekend when my wife and I decided to have chicken for dinner and we bought two rather expensive packets of "fresh" chicken breast, which according to the printed date, had been packed put on sale that morning.

At home my wife proceeded to wash the chicken and soon called me as she noticed that when she was washing the chicken, the flesh was virtually melting on her hands and being washed out in the sink.

Not that chicken flesh usually melts no matter how strong you are or how strong your press, but with her 42 kg of weight I doubt that my wife has the strength to manage that. More likely, the supplier decided to cut costs by using some chemicals in pass the date chicken and put it on the counter as fresh one, while not even offering a discount!

Needless to say that the chicken ended up in the bin, and we had to change our dinner plans.

After doing some surveying on facebook (great place in Vietnam to find honest and not so honest answers), it seems that in order to save costs Big C has got rid of almost all foreign managers, which means that quality control has fallen in the hands of Vietnamese whose concept of quality is based in the normal Vietnamese way of buying chicken: going to the local market where people who bought the chicken from the farmers earlier in the morning, killed them, cleaned them and kept them on the street (around 36 to 40 degrees) with no ice, no refrigeration, lots of flies around, no clean knives, to health inspectors, no nothing…until being sold.

Again the Big Con may be saving money by paying lower salaries for local managers, and no having hardly any quality control, however how long before the people revert to local markets as they find out that the more expensive prices that we pay for "safe" products in Big C is just, a big con?

WHY NOT: have good quality standards that reflect the prices you charge, rather than just cutting corners and putting your Customers' health at risk?

In Vietnam we get so many scandals about food scams (from plastic noodles, to coffee made with no coffee beans), but what will happen to the Casino Group's reputation if this gets released to the French press? Should I write to the French newspapers? Tempted!

Hoan My Hospital (Vietnam)

Hoan My is one of the many private hospitals that have opened their doors in Vietnam over the last few years, offering better health care, or so they claim, than the national hospitals, appealing for the better health care demand and income of the emerging middle classes.

Some time ago I woke up with a terrible stiff neck, so painful, that any small movement in the wrong direction would make me scream.

As I could not do much under such situation, not to mention driving, I decided to go to my closest hospital, Hoan My, rather than to An Sinh my favourite one but requiring more driving.

So on arrival I went to reception, and I brought my wife because even though staff and doctors are supposed to speak English, I did not want to take any chance of misunderstandings.

After explaining the problem in reception, I insisted to see a physiotherapist, but they told me that I had to be seen by a different doctor first (obviously a receptionist knows better than me…), but pain is king, so I paid the fee and we went to the doctor's office.

After waiting outside, the nurse invited us to the consultation room, where both my wife and I explained the problem to the doctor who took a little hammer and proceeded to softly hit me in the hand, arm, elbow, knee, and leg.

I repeatedly reminded him that my pain was in the back of my neck, but he ignored both my wife and me, and without even having a look at my neck asked us to take an x-ray.

So we went back to reception to pay for the x-ray, as you will not get any service unless you pay for it in advance, we were then directed to the x-ray area, where we waited patiently for over 15 minutes with no one on site.

We tried opening the door, no luck, and finally 25 minutes later someone appeared so we asked. She told us that we had to wait there just five more minutes. Ten minutes later someone else appeared, and please bear in mind that the pain during this time is increasing so each second feels like an hour, not to mention the frustration, and this person asked us to wait, again.

A few minutes later another nurse appeared who told us to go for lunch because the x-ray people would be at lunch from 12 to 1, and the department did not work during those hours.

I looked at my watch, told her that not only was not 12 yet, but that we had been there waiting for 45 minutes, to which she responded that I could do whatever I wanted but no one would take my x-ray until after 1. So I made a very nice paper ball with my invoice and I gave to her, I then took my wife to my favourite hospital, where I was properly seen, x-rayed and treated.

HOW ON HELL in a private hospital where people pay a premium for service, you have the full x-ray department leaving together for lunch, not to mention that they leave for a considerably extended lunch, with no notice no information, but total disregards for their Customers and their health.

Even though this hospital is more centrally located than An Sinh, they have many less Customers, not to mention that their reputation keeps worsening, but that is easy to understand, isn't it?

Starting with reception, I am the Customer and I know what I want, and I am paying for it, why cant I have it? It is not that I am asking for something illegal, is it? And although I am not a medical doctor, I am sure that my knowledge of medicine, not to mention knowing my own symptoms, is much better of that of a receptionist.

The Doctor, and I am sure that checking my reflexes gave him a lot of information, should not have had a look at the neck, as the doctor at the other hospital did, who although also requested an x-ray to ensure she gave me the right diagnose, already told me the likely cause.

Vietnam Airlines

Vietnam Airlines is the national airline of Vietnam which is expected soon to be privatised, or at least partly. Being the most expensive to fly with in Vietnam, it is colloquially known as "Sorry Airlines", because they keep apologising for their many cock ups rather than doing something to avoid them.

Although they mostly employ foreign pilots, the ground operations are 100% Vietnamese run, and the result is obvious: virtually every flight is either delayed or cancelled, rescheduled and ground services are terrible at their best.

In my first trip back to England with my wife, I did not want a long flight, and Vietnam Airlines was the only one offering a direct flight between HCMC and London, so I decided to pay the premium and enjoy a direct flight frills free, right!

A few weeks before departure date I received an email from Sorry Airlines, saying that they were sorry but they had to change my flight schedule; this situation was repeated three times more, until the last time, just a few days before departure when my direct flight to London would now stop in Germany for refuelling.

You do not need to know much about planes to know that it was a lie, and later on this was confirmed unofficially when I met a Sorry Airlines pilot who told me that they do this all the time: when a flight does not have many passenger, in order to reduce costs they cancel it or re-direct to another country, great.

The flight left late, and that was just the beginning of the nightmare. To start with, at least half of the toilets were not working, so if usually is annoying to use the toilet in a long haul flight imagine if less than half are available.

The so called entertainment system lasted for one hour, not a big issue for me as I was relying on my tablet and laptop for killing time, however it makes you think that if they are unable to maintain two simple thing like toilets and tvs, what about engines, navigation systems,...better not to think.

The food was dreadful, but nothing compared to the (lack of) service of the queens and kings of the airline, who as airhostess they seem to have forgotten that they are being employed to help and serve the Customers.

Just before we landed in Frankfurt, the Captain informed us about the landing, the need to leave the plane, and that we had to go through airport security again,... It was then obvious that I had been one of the few lucky passengers who had been informed in advance (or at least read) about the flight's stop over.

Many people started to panic as having just s single entry visa to England, which does not cover Schengen states like Germany, could get them in trouble and they did not know what would happen.

Two hours later, after leaving the plane, going through customs and passport control, we joined a different plane and flight and an hour later we landed in Gatwick Airport.

WHY NOT respect the terms of the contract, if you offer a direct flight you should run a direct flight. When they make extra profit companies do not give anything back to Customers, so why should Customers be penalised when the airlines do not do enough business?

WHY NOT ensure minimum maintenance of toilets, entertainment systems, and everything. Especially if you advertise so much luxury, amenities, etc. in the flights. And if you don't deliver as promised, why not pay back/compensate the Customers?

Since this experience and that of the return flight which was similar, I have avoided Vietnam Airlines, even if as a result I have to pay more or fly longer, and I am very happy about it!

Vietnam Airlines Ground Services

On my last business trip to Hong Kong I decided to fly with Cathay Pacific. Unfortunately and due to the political tensions at the time between Vietnam and China, they decided to cancel most of their flights, and on my return, my Cathay Pacific flight was converted into a Vietnam Airlines flight, my luck.

As usual the plane was late, on arrival to HCMC they kept as flying around for one hour, apparently due to a storm, though at that altitude everything was on sight and the sun was shining, and I am not so sure to which point, if a storm is dangerous, it is safer to be kept on the air rather that attempt landing.

Anyway, after one hour of flying in circles we landed in Tan Son Nhat Airport in HCMC. For once I was lucky, and no only there were not long queues in immigration but also Mr policeman was quick rather than the usual nonsense.

So still enjoying the sunshine I went to the luggage area to wait for my luggage, time in which it started raining, may be the famous storm had finally arrived, but we were during rainy season when it rains almost every day!

Well, we waited and waited and not a single suitcase arrived in 45 minutes, so I saw far away someone working for the airport, and I asked her who automatically and without checking replied that luggage would arrive soon. But how soon is soon?

At that time another passenger, a guy from Australia which was quite irritated, joined me in the questioning, and then the girl, took as to see the supervisor who told us that we had to wait because it was raining and the luggage employees did not want to get wet. Unbelievable.

Both the Australian guy and I tried to reason with him about the inadequacy of having hundreds of people waiting for already one hour just because a few twats refused to get wet to do their job.

Threats followed, and the result was that then an official announcement was made that the airport had been closed because there was a VIP flying out. An obvious lie in order to keep us calm, but it just managed to get the opposite.

WHY NOT put the Customer first, and consider what is right, rather that what is convenient for some lazy employees. Imagine the chaos, of having the passengers from several international flights packed together, and then trying to leave the airport at the same, a small airport.

Jet Star Pacific

Jet Star Pacific is another Vietnamese airline co-own by Vietnam Airlines and Australian Qantas.

I decided to fly with them on my first trip to Hanoi, a leisure trip to discover the capital of Vietnam.

Although the flight between HCMC and Hanoi was relatively smooth, apart from the usual 45 minutes delay of course, on the way back it was hell.

A few hours before flying I received a text message, in Vietnamese only, saying that due to overbooking if I was still planning to fly (on the flight that I have already fully paid) I had to go as soon as possible to one of their offices to check in and get a ticket on top of my online reservation.

So my wife and I had to cancel our sightseeing plans and get on our way to Jet Star Pacific office which was more or less a room manned by two idiots and two security people.

A long queue of passengers carrying all sorts of items, including livestock, waited patiently to be served, and when it was our turn, everybody was looking at us, as I was the only foreigner, the racist son of… of Jet Star Pacific representative decided to create trouble and told my wife that she could not travel with her little suitcase as hand luggage as it was too big.

Logic did not win, nor the reasoning that we had used that very suitcase to fly with the same airline. In a rather rude way he told us to check the luggage (for which we had to go to the airport with no ticket) and pay extra, or not fly.

So I decided to solve the problem, and I put my wife's case on the floor, and I kicked it twice to break the side handle, which was the reason why this idiot argumented that the suitcase was too big.

He started then shouting asking me to leave and called security who threatened me to arrest me if I continue to break (my own) suitcase.

At that time I had already had enough so I turned back to the two guys (airlines rep plus security) and I clearly told them what is was obvious: I was doing nothing wrong, and if they dared to touch me they better think it twice as I was bigger than them two together and the first to lie a hand on me would kiss the floor. Plus I reminded them that they had no legal power to arrest me or anyone.

I was "allowed" to finish taking the side handle off, I got the tickets, but then we had to wait in the airport for several hours because… see next chapter.

WHY NOT put the Customer first, and consider what is right, rather that be racist and put your personal interests and views first.

Why be unreasonable with your Customers, especially when they are doing nothing wrong. Have you forgotten that you have a job and that you get paid a salary thanks to your Customers?

Viet Jet Air

Once we reached the airport after our adventure with Jet Star Pacific, we realised that there was a total mess at the airport.

Due to apparently bad weather conditions in the middle of the country, there was a huge delay in most flights, with many Vietnam Airlines flights cancelled, all Jet Star Pacific delayed, and rumours of cancellation.

After several hours seeing that flight after flight form these airlines was being cancelled on the screen, and with both my wife and I having to be back in HCMC to work the following day, we decided to book an expensive flight with the other only available company, Viet Jet Air, which although with delay, were still managing to fly their planes.

So we booked online using my laptop and we had then tickets for two flights which were delayed, but flying within 10 minutes of each other.

I had by then frequently asked the gate ladies from Jet Star Pacific about our original flight, so when I did the same with the ladies from Viet Jet Air, who have obviously noticed me, they told me that I could not fly with two companies at the same time.

And then we entered into a long discussion, my reasoning being that legally, even though I cannot be physically in two different planes, I can book and pay for, for as many flights I want as it is my money, and as they were so incompetent and I needed to be back in HCMC I had bought two flights and I would take the first one leaving Hanoi, assuming any of them would leave.

WHY NOT try to help your Customer, and if you do not know about something, why assume and behave as if you were right, when you are just assuming, and usually assuming wrong.

Skagen

I want to dedicate this, the last example of terrible Customer Service, to Skagen, a company which qualifies as a real cowboy of luxury goods, bought two years ago by Fossil Inc (USA).

On my last trip to England I decided to treat my wife and I to new watches, and although I have never been into expensive watches I decided to make an exception and I bought a beautifully designed Skagen watch at Stanstead Airport (London), before our flight to Spain to visit my parents; my wife was more clever and she chose Tissot.

Although the design was beautiful and stylish, what really convinced me to buy the watch was the International lifetime guarantee.

I do not expect a watch to last forever, but when I am paying several hundred dollars for one, I want to have the peace of mind that it will last a few years.

It lasted four days.

When I was in Spain the watch stopped working, and I went through a cumbersome web system to email different addresses from Skagen requesting for assistance to repair or replace my brand new watch.

They did not have a Skagen branch in the city I was at the time, and they asked me to either send it back to the UK or send it to the US; it would take them several weeks to repair it, and they could send it back to me to Vietnam.

The problem with that, is that any packet sent to Vietnam will be opened by Customs, inspected, with contents quite often stolen or replaced by a fake or by stones, and in any case I would be subject to 100% import tax, which I was not willing to pay.

As I was planning to go back to London before I flew to Vietnam, and as they had several retailers in London on top of on all London's airports, I suggested to Skagen to take my watch to one of their retailers to get it replaced or repair quick as I would only stay in London for three more days, but they refused.

I then suggested to get the watch replaced or repaired by their distributor in HCMC, but they told me that I should take it to Hanoi, where their main service center was.

At that time I had had enough of such an overpriced, poor quality, zero Customer support company and I reminded them of what the Sale of Goods and Services Act says under these circumstances, which applied as I had bought the watch on British soil, I also reminded them of the possibility of going public and inform people about the quality they can expected if they buy Skagen products.

No reply, so I decided to cut my losses and take the watch to my local jeweller who within minutes opened the watch, changed the battery and gave it back to me working.

A week letter I received an email from Skagen saying that they agreed for me to take the watch for repair to HCMC.

Three months later, back in Vietnam, I was careless enough to drop my watch into the floor: I had left it on top of a chair, about 50 cm high, dropped into the floor and the watch's glass got a nick, what terrible quality!

I have had many Casio and Seiko watches, way less expensive than Skagen, dropped several times or even have accidents with them, never a scratch!

I then decided to take the Skagen watch to the Official Retailer to change the glass, and after agreeing the price, they told me that I had to leave the watch there for a week, as they needed to order the watch from another city.

I then asked the guy to order the glass and ring me when it arrived so I could bring the watch but he refused because, as I was a foreigner, he did not trust that I would come back. Nothing works better than being so nice to Customers!

I decided to live with an expensive watch, with a little nick on the glass, and which soon started to lose colour on the strap.

Over the last few days the time on the watch was slowing down, perhaps the battery, but more likely the watch, so yesterday I decided to go to one of the best shopping centers and I bought myself a beloved Cassio, which if the quality follows that I have experienced in the past, will last me for a long time.

WHY NOT: make products whose quality matches the high price. If you are charging a lot of money for high quality, deliver it!

If you offer a worldwide lifetime guarantee, aiming at convincing Customers to buy, why not honour it.

This was my first and last Skagen watch, and I really felt relief when yesterday I took it off and put it on a box.

WHY NOT: how companies can do things better, much better, for their Customers, and indirectly for themselves

Here you will find all my final recommendations for each of the previous cases.

You do not need to read them again, but it can be useful not only as a reminder, but also aimed to those who want just to have access to best practice.

WHAT IF: what if, Panrico on receipt of my mum's first letter had answered on the lines of "Sorry to have kept you waiting for your toy, but we did not receive your coupons. Nevertheless as we value you as a customer, here is your toy!

By doing this, they would have reinforced so much my, and my mum's loyalty to Panrico. Instead we got angry, stop buying their products, and shared our "experience" with other mums and school children… try to measure the effect.

WHY NOT: once they rang and found out that I was too young, why not give their personal details and encourage my mum to contact them once I was old enough to do these courses.

They would have created a good image, rather than a terrible one, plus I would have had a good memory of this company, and something to look forward, rather than put them in my "black list", and over 30 years after, I have not forgotten!

WHY NOT: test the printer and everything and make sure all works before leaving.

Why not send the technician to the Customer's home, rather than annoy the Customer with bringing the product to the company? I know is easier and cheaper for the company, however who is serving who?

Why not replace the printer immediately, the Customer paid for a working one! So rather than transfer the problem to the Customer, accept it, and make him happy, that is the quality he (I) paid for!

WHY NOT: deal with the repairs yourself? If you don't trust the Customer, why don't use your own approved technicians rather than pass the ball to the customer and ask to do work for you for free?

WHY NOT apologise? Why not listen to the Customer and start from the base that the Customer is (always) right?

Just because I was young it does not mean that they know better than me, but even if they did, they should still respect me as a Customer.

WHY NOT treat Customers with respect to start with, and take the few seconds that it takes to check the statement in the computer and give an explanation.

Someone, not the Customer, made a big mistake, there was no apology, and no compensation or goodwill gesture for the time or stress caused.

WHY NOT: explain clearly any charges to Customers, rather than bleeding them in as many ways as possible?

With such short term view, it is not abnormal that so many people change banks!

WHY NOT acknowledge the importance of timed documents. If they did not know what the address was, why not ask for help from the Customer rather than ask the Customer to return after two weeks and do nothing about it during such time, why not deal with the issue.

What would have happened if I had lost my money due to their incompetence?

WHY NOT: even if a Customer does not pay the last bill, why not ring him, at least to warn him/her are discontinuing the service?

Why punish a Customer, for something he is not at all responsible for.

WHY NOT trust a Customer, I was not asking for credit, or even a credit card, I was just asking for a basic account to put my money, in fact a rather large amount of money. Why not trust the officially signed and stamped Bank letters?

Years later the same bank would approach me on a regular basis offering bank accounts, credit cards, loans, mortgages, everything… but I did not forget how I was treated by them, and I will never will!

WHY NOT help your Customer? The UK branch could easily access my banking records in Spain for building my credit scoring or ask the Spanish branch for my credit scoring… it was easier to do nothing and not Care for the Customer.

Soon after I cancelled my card, and I have not done any business with Citibank since.

If meeting Customers' expectations is great, exceeding them is definitely the way to Customer loyalty and succeed in business.

WHY NOT honour what you say and offer "real" on site service. Who would be willing to wait seven weeks, or even seven days to have a computer repaired?

Why pass the responsibility and even costs to the Customer when he is not responsible for anything apart from giving his money and business to a rogue trader? Eclipse computers ended up losing an order, losing a Customer, paying for couriers, and probably blacklisted by American Express.

On the other hand American Express reinforced the satisfaction of a Customer by once more exceeding his expectations, a Customer who has been recommending Amex ever since.

WHY NOT deliver on time, which is why you get extra money.

Why lie to the Customer? Why create more problems for the Customer rather than solve them?

WHY NOT ensure the registration system works, and if problems arise, when they don't?, listen to the Customer and use the logic to assess whether the claim is or is not reasonable.

They had 2 months of my custom, and never again more, plus zero recommendations to friends, but the opposite.

Why so often do companies employ people with zero Customer Service skills and below zero communication skills in roles with direct contact with Customers? I wonder…

WHY NOT: why not inform the Customer of any changes in any agreement, it has been a long time since doctors can give 15 minute slots to patients, so why Customers are forced to take days off work, not being able to leave their houses, simply because these rogue companies decide to take the easy way, not to mention when there is no wrong doing from the Customers.

Why lie to Customers and treat them as if they were stupid? And if things go pear shape, why not compensate Customers fairly for the damage done.

Had I been offered £150-200 I would have been satisfied, but £10? What an insult! At the end the company ended paying me a couple of thousands, not to mention their legal costs.

WHY NOT: try to solve the problems of a loyal Customer, listen to him, and try to do what is right.

Why not try to investigate and see whose fault is it, and in any case try to solve the situation and care about the Customers, who are actually paying the salaries of the employees?

By the way, it was never clarified who had ordered the phones, as Orange was unable to provide any proof of me or anyone else having even placed an order…

WHY NOT: deliver what you promise to the Customers, or stop over selling services, or actually cheating, people are not stupid!

Why not return calls when you promise to do so, why ignore emails and faxes.

And more important, in a market with many providers, if you stop a service, especially a service which costs you nothing, as a result of the Customer withholding payments because he is being ignored, do you think that anyone would pay, when they can simply go to another supplier?

I moved to Vodafone, with who many years after I keep a contract with, without a single problem!

WHY NOT: If there is a restriction in a contract, why not inform the Customer in advance, and let him decide whether to accept it or not. Business will go only so far if Customers feel being cheated.

WHY NOT: take responsibility for the products you sell. Customers can deal directly with the manufacturers, but so can you, and at the end of the day you are making the profit, remember Customers can also take their business somewhere else, and we do!

WHY NOT: take responsibility for defects and empathise with the Customer.

If you provide a low quality faulty product, that is followed by terrible, service do you think Customers will buy from you again?

WHY NOT: be honest with the Customer and explain every single term to them, especially those which are likely to result in damage for the Customer.

WHY: why threat your Customers, especially by assuming that they have done something wrong? Why not talk to them, why not ask and enquire to see if there is a problem, or simply some miscommunication?

Unfortunately over the years this would be a norm from Hackney employees who without exception behaved unprofessionally, threatening and were nothing but spoilt bullies as they are covered/protected by a public body, which by the way, should be taking care of people rather than harassing them.

WHY NOT: treat the Customer respectfully and believe what he says to start with.

WHY NOT: honour the offers, rather than trick Customers.

HOWEVER: very well done last department about apologising, finding facts, and compensating gesture for the Customer.

WHY NOT: take responsibility and help the Customers, rather than pass the ball on, especially when you are taking their money?

WHY: why cant other companies learn from such wonderful service, attitude and well doing as National Grid provides. Sometimes is great to be a Customer!

WHY NOT: respect the contracts and agreements with Customers.

WHY NOT: tell the truth to Customers, rather than treating them like idiots.

WHY NOT: honour the deal and respect it.

WHY: cheat on your Customers who are bringing you business.

WHY NOT: be decent, honest and do business the right way, according to the law, especially if you are a big multinational company.

Guess what, Iberia has been having tremendous losses, I keep hearing horror stories, I do not know many people who would fly with them, time for them to disappear.

WHY NOT: honour what you agree with Customers, and if you have two people traveling together and seats are available, allocate them properly; and if you don't want to do so, don't promise!

WHY NOT: have enough meals of the most likely meal to be ordered. Which percentage of the population flying from London is likely to be vegetarian? Do you ever think?

WHY NOT: inform passengers if there is an issue, no matter how minor, on board, especially when they can see something happening, and panic is not good.

WHY NOT: take responsibility if you screw it up, like breaking your Customer's property, do you really think that it is fair that you break someone luggage and you ask them to solve the problem, rather than either solving it yourself, of buying new one on the spot?

WHY NOT: honour your part of the contract.

WHY: make up new, silly stupid, rules. And

WHY: bother your Customers with preparing lots of documentation if you already know the value of the item and you do not plan to pay.

The answer, I guess, is that rogue companies here abuse, hoping that Customers will not take them to Court, and that most Customers will not keep all the un-necessary papers. Ombudsman, where are you?

WHY: companies can not learn from such simple, but great ways to operate like this. It is simple, straight forward and fair for everyone, and most important, keeps Customers loyal!

WHY NOT: be fair, and rather than be greedy and expect your Customers to cover your expenses due to poor management, take responsibility for your own deeds.

WHY NOT: use logic and respect your Customers. Was it really necessary to increase the insurance fee 15% on top of the 10% already increased just because I was one day late in accepting?

WHY: when you are doing something well, and make money with it, not keep doing it (or even improving it). AXA learn!

WHY NOT: check if the Customer is right when he/she complains?

Why not give Customers the benefit of the doubt, and why insult Customers? All unnecessary never leading to anything good.

WHY: why kick out Customers, especially if they are on time? Why drive business away, especially considering that there were not doing much business at the time, rather than be grateful for having extra income.

WHY NOT: answer correspondence from your Customers, not to mention you shareholders, they take the time to give you vital information to improve, and you ignore it rather than being grateful?

WHY NOT: be honest and charge what you advertise rather than trick your Customers. People are not stupid, and they do not like to be robbed!

WHY NOT: be clear with your Customers and try to explain, in simple terms, all the options and the implications of them, rather than tricking them. This is so wrong…

WHY NOT: be clear with your Customers and try to explain, in simple terms, all the options and the implications of them, rather than tricking them.

Especially when the Customer is requesting the most beneficial option for him, why try to convince him to do something that will result in the Customer being worse off?

WHY: always blame the Customer, who is who brings money to companies, rather than investigating and taking ownerships of their own mistakes.

WHY NOT: respect your Customers' wishes, why break the law, and why force Customers to pay for products that they do not want, and which they have not asked to buy?

WHY NOT: listen to your Customer and do some research, rather than assume that the Customer is lying?

WHY: not honour your part of the contract, when you expect Customers to honour theirs, especially considering that in the UK if you are found to be traveling without a valid ticket you commit a crime and could easily end with a criminal record. Unfair that the strict law seems to be applied to only on side

WHY NOT: provide excellent service when possible, especially considering the absurd high costs that passengers have to pay when traveling using public transport in London, and especially considering that when the service is substandard (which is most of the times), you still charge the same to passengers. Unfair!

WHY NOT: do your job and investigate faults, rather than expect them to get solved by themselves, and rather than blaming the Customer (or in this case, my computers) try to find and solve the reason for the fault.

WHY NOT: consider your Customers and the effect on them when considering major changes.

And if you go ahead with changes why not inform your Customers in advance, so they know what to expect.

And one week to send an engineer? Why not a month or a year!

WHY NOT: honour the part of the deal without hidden charges. Why try to impose unrequested guarantees and services on your Customers, knowing that many will not be bothered to cancel, this is nothing but fraud!

WHY NOT: admit mistakes? And in particular if you make them, make sure to correct them. Whether the waitress forgot to order the prawns to the kitchen (four times!) or whether it was the kitchen who forgot, live with it, if the Customer asks you to cancel a dish, especially one which is 90 minutes late, and that you have probably not even started cooking, learn from it.

WHY blame the Customer, why lie, and why accuse and pass the blame to the Customer? If you make a mistake, start by apologising, and try to correct it and learn from it.

WHY NOT use valuable feedback. Companies should reward Customers who take the time to complain, as they are giving them free great feedback about their products and services. Wishing them good luck next time, is like telling them to f*** off, and they will!

WHY NOT call the Customer immediately if you have a problem with a money transfer.

WHY blame the Customer, when it is obvious that all the details are correct

WHY not let someone close their own account, or make it so difficult, just to keep a large number of unused accounts open, and show that you have so many (fictional) Customers?

WHY NOT check with Customers first before imposing a new service (or product) which they had not requested.

WHY not follow the Customer's desire to cancel a service, especially considering that the Customer did not request it.

WHY NOT make products of such quality that justifies the high price.

WHY NOT make repairs at reasonable prices, rather than charge more for a replacement than for a new one.

WHY NOT: learn from companies, that although young, exceed in understanding Customers and serving them.

WHY NOT make product of such quality that justifies the high price.

WHY NOT make repairs at reasonable prices, rather than charge more for a replacement than for a new one.

WHY NOT check that basic things like water and clean sheets are available, on a daily basis, but especially when having new guests?

WHY NOT knock on someone doors and wait for him/her to open before entering, it is basic education, isn't it?

WHY lie to the Customer, by first using different size standards (saving just a few cms of material), then guaranteeing the standards as international, ensuring that I can return within one week but then refusing to accept the return. Yes, they got my money that day but never again, not to mention the large amount of people that I have convinced not to buy from them. In the long term they lose rather than win!

WHY not trust your Customers unless they give you a real reason not to. Was it my fault that the voucher was broken, you could say I was sloppy and the mix of me being fat, weather hot, no aircon and the razor thin paper used to make it resulted in it getting easily broken.

However the vouchers are numbered and coded, they make you sign in a book when they give it to you, so it was not difficult to check that first, that voucher was real, and second that no one had used it, but why help and serve the Customer? And more important why accuse the Customer of fraud, especially if innocent.

WHY NOT think about your Customer first? Try to put yourself in your Customers' shoes and see how changes that you impose on them my affect them.

WHY NOT spend some time thinking about what can go wrong, what Customers may need, and provide it straight away and before hand.

WHY NOT trust your Customers rather than assume that they are there to steal from you.

How many people are likely to buy or do business with someone who without reason already suspects them to be criminals, I will not, and not many people will.

Would not be easier to respect your Customers, to expect them not to steal, as I am sure is the case with 99% of them, and if needed increase the number of cameras, security personnel, or simply ask to show their bags at the end of the shopping experience.

WHY NOT: have good quality standards that reflect the prices you charge, rather than just cutting corners and putting your Customers' health at risk?

In Vietnam we get so many scandals about food scams (from plastic noodles, to coffee made with no coffee beans), but what will happen to the Casino Group's reputation if this gets released to the French press? Should I write to the French newspapers? Tempted!

HOW ON HELL in a private hospital where people pay a premium for service, you have the full x-ray department leaving together for lunch, not to mention that they leave for a considerably extended lunch, with no notice no information, but total disregards for their Customers and their health.

WHY NOT respect the terms of the contract, if you offer a direct flight you should run a direct flight. When they make extra profit companies do not give anything back to Customers, so why should Customers be penalised when the airlines do not do enough business?

WHY NOT ensure minimum maintenance of toilets, entertainment systems, and everything. Especially if you advertise so much luxury, amenities, etc. in the flights. And if you don't deliver as promised, why not pay back/compensate the Customers?

WHY NOT put the Customer first, and consider what is right, rather that what is convenient for some lazy employees. Imagine the chaos, of having the passengers from several international flights packed together, and then trying to leave the airport at the same, a small airport.

WHY NOT put the Customer first, and consider what is right, rather that be racist and put your personal interests and views first.

Why be unreasonable with your Customers, especially when they are doing nothing wrong. Have you forgotten that you have a job and that you get paid a salary thanks to your Customers?

WHY NOT try to help your Customer, and if you do not know about something, why assume and behave as if you were right, when you are just assuming, and usually assuming wrong.

WHY NOT: make products whose quality matches the high price. If you are charging a lot of money for high quality, deliver it!

If you offer a worldwide lifetime guarantee, aiming at convincing Customers to buy, why not honour it.

This was my first and last Skagen watch, and I really felt relief when yesterday I took it off and put it on a box.

Also from this Author

Ho Chi Minh City (Saigon) best restaurants

Fine dining at a fraction of Western prices

Alfredo de la Casa

Vietnam is a fascinating country, still unspoilt by mass tourism unlike some nearby countries, and although there are several guides already published (including one from the author of this book), they tend to concentrate in the main attractions, most of which are concentrated in the city centre, while ignoring some of the beauties, which although not far away from the centre, hardly see any foreign face.

From the awarded author of "Saigon 2013: Guide to Ho Chi Minh City", and "Vietnam Business and people, understanding to cultural differences" comes this new guide book to help you discover some hidden gems in Ho Chi Minh City, giving you the opportunity to observe and experience real life of Vietnamese people.

What will you find in this book:

How to screw your Customers – Alfredo de la Casa

- Very interesting hidden temples, covering the many religions practised in Vietnam.

- How to reach the suggested sites from the city centre.

- Time to reach them, and how much a taxi will cost.

- Suggestions for best eats nearby.

- Daily real life of Vietnamese.

- Markets where Vietnamese shop (Ben Thanh market is for tourist only!) at Vietnamese prices.

- Lots of pictures and maps.

- Suggested walking itineraries, and time to do them.

- Up to date information as per January 2014.

What will NOT find in this book:

- Touristic places appearing in popular guide books, ok just a couple or so reviewed.

- History of Vietnam (there are many books already about it).

- Information about expensive or rip off restaurants.

- Photos of the interior of the temples: I am not religious, but it is a matter of respect.

With this book, and using my experience in settling in Viet Nam, I try to help future expats or even tourists to make the most out of Viet Nam, with minimum difficulties to achieve their objectives, this being to communicate with a pharmacist or the lucky money protocol in Tet. I am also including a lot of information on cultural differences, as problems can easily be reached without knowing due to some drastic cultural differences between Vietnamese ways and Western ways. I have divided the book in small chapters so that it is easy to find various subjects. The book can be read in any order as each chapter is independent. I hope you find it helpful and enjoy reading it!

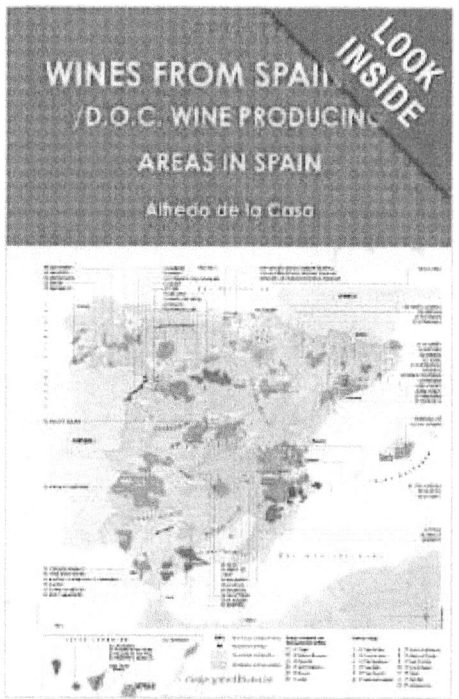

A concise easy to read book with information of all the wine producing areas in Spain, including description of the various origin denominations, grapes, production surface and much more.

I could write a lot about what I think you should see and visit around Malaysia, however, an image is better than a thousand words, and here I am presenting you with over 340 pictures of beautiful Malaysia, which I am sure are better than 340.000 words, for you to see, judge and hopefully encourage you to visit Malaysia

In this book I am presenting my favourite 99 restaurants around London. I love eating, I love eating good food even more, and if I have to pay little for it and a good service is provided, that is what I call perfection. It is not very difficult to find a good restaurant serving good food if you are willing to pay £70 or more per person. This book is not about that type of eateries, but the opposite: after having lived for 13 years in London I have tried many restaurants, some good some not so good, here I have collated those I think you should try, with a special mention to my top 10 favourites.

How to screw your Customers – Alfredo de la Casa

Simple! This book is about how you can live in Vietnam, having a great life for just $300 a month, plus how to easily get that amount of money by working around 10-12 hours a month, are you tempted?

Ok, let's make a few things clear:

This is not a miracle book, or in other words, you do not need to make short of a miracle to achieve such living! This is easily achievable by virtually anyone, as long as your English is good enough.costs listed here are real at the time of writing (May 2013) and they are likely to stay similar for a while.book does not require you to live under a bridge or do something illegal to achieve the living standards, is just normal living, normal costs, you just need to drink beer in Vietnamese restaurants (50 cents or less for a cold one) rather than in ex-pat bars ($3-$7).prices, and places are real! I am a fully qualified Chartered Management Accountant, so I know about numbers!will need to make some changes to your diet, however that does not mean that you will starve or that your diet will be limited to rice. Vietnamese food is delicious (and I have even gained 7 kilos here), what it means is that you may need to say goodbye to olives or cherries (which are imported products and expensive) and welcome fresh fish, oysters, prawns, mangoes, coconuts,... which are grown locally and terribly cheap.

In this book I will tell you what is cool and nice, like semi-deserted beaches, and what is not so good or terrible, like traffic, so that you have a realistic picture of life here before you decide whether to move here or not.

I am also attaching two little presents: Cultural and business guide to Vietnamto Ho Chi Minh City and other major cities and tourist destinations.

I am sure you will enjoy reading, and may be I will be drinking a beer next to you if you move to Vietnam!

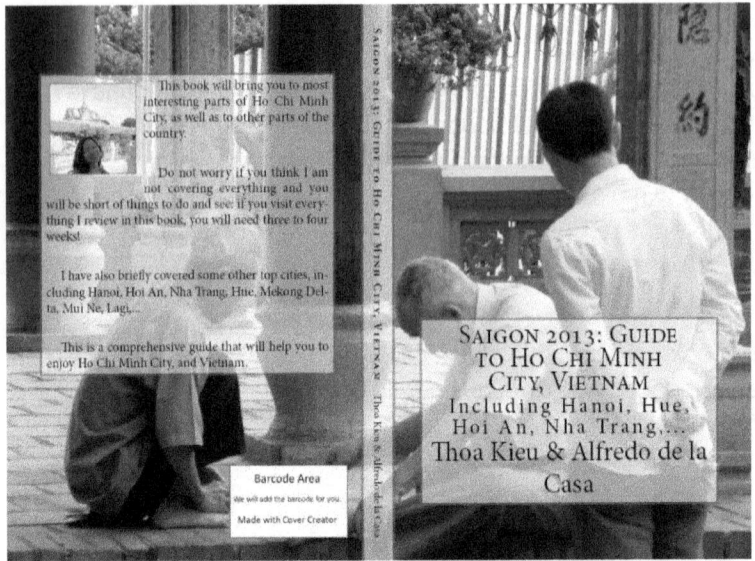

www.ingramcontent.com/pod-product-compliance
Lightning Source LLC
Chambersburg PA
CBHW071423170526
45165CB00001B/378